NEW LONDON ARCHITECTURE

KENNETH POWELL

NEW LONDON ARCHITECTURE

MERRELL

Published by Merrell Publishers Limited
42 Southwark Street
London SE1 1UN

Telephone +44 (0)20 7403 2047
E-mail mail@merrellpublishers.com

Publisher Hugh Merrell
Editorial Director Julian Honer
Art Director Matthew Hervey
Sales and Marketing Director Mark Beken

First published 2001

Distributed in the USA and Canada by Rizzoli International
Publications, Inc. through St Martin's Press, 175 Fifth Avenue,
New York, New York 10010

British Library Cataloguing-in-Publication Data:
Powell, Kenneth, 1947–
New London architecture
1.Architecture, Modern – 20th century – England – London
2.Buildings – England – London – History – 20th century
3.London (England) – Buildings, structures etc. – History –
20th century
I.Title
720.9'421'09049

ISBN 1 85894 150 4

Designed by Maggi Smith
Edited by Mary Ore and Sarah Kane

Printed and bound by Eurolitho S.p.a., Cesano Boscone (Milan), Italy.

ACKNOWLEDGEMENTS

I am grateful to Hugh Merrell and Julian Honer at Merrell Publishers for having the courage to take on this
book and the stamina and patience to see it through to completion. Thanks are due to all the practices who
provided images and information for the book and to the many architects who took time to discuss their
projects with me. The selection of projects is a personal one and exclusion should not be seen as negative –
though in some cases we had to drop schemes because practices failed to supply the material required,
despite many reminders.

Encouragement and advice came from many quarters and from many friends, both architects and critics.
In particular I should especially like to thank Isabel Allen and Paul Finch for commenting on the project list
and suggesting additions, some of them inspirational. Roland Paoletti and Tom Muirhead were further
sources of wisdom. I should also like to thank Yvonne Jordan and her colleagues at VIEW for their generous
and enthusiastic help with the sometimes daunting task of sourcing suitable photographs for this book.

Finally, I should like to dedicate this book to the staff of the London Underground, which has carried me
around London for many years and remains the capital's greatest and most undervalued asset.

Kenneth Powell
London, 2001

CONTENTS

The view from Tower 42 across London: a commercial metropolis in constant change, with the Thames as its central artery

London is a world city where architecture can rarely be discussed without politics, to some degree, intruding. Unlike Paris, Rome, Madrid or Berlin, London has been a commercial, trading city for much of its history. Most of the other leading business cities of Europe – Frankfurt, Milan and Amsterdam, for example – are not capitals. London's character bears the memories of a court-versus-commerce tension that extends back five hundred years; hence the two cities of London and Westminster and the lack of grand piazzas, processional avenues and monumental regal architecture. London is not only a political and commercial capital, it is also, by European standards at least, still a metropolis, with a large population and strong industrial roots. Its economy is equivalent to that of smaller member states of the European Union. Heathrow Airport generates more wealth than entire provincial cities. Yet London has, until recently, lacked a city government: the prostitution of its County Hall to a mix of commercial uses (including an aquarium) bewilders foreigners. County Hall's successor, the Greater London Authority headquarters at London Bridge City, is an impressive and innovative structure, yet it is effectively a spin-off from an office development. London's confident, even expansive, mood in the early years of the twenty-first century – it may yet be punctured by recession – comes after several decades of self-doubt and despondency. "Is London dying?" asked the *Evening Standard* in August 1991: "filthy, clogged and dangerous streets" and a population "increasingly homeless, unemployed and desperate" reflected its crisis. There was a good deal of journalistic hyperbole in all this, but Londoners were genuinely beginning to feel that their city was not what it was – hadn't the Underground once been the envy of the world? Infrastructural and architectural issues figured prominently in London's fight-back. In 1992, during the run-up to a general election in which the Labour Party's hopes were to be dashed, Richard Rogers, not yet a Labour peer, and Labour's shadow arts minister Mark Fisher published

A New London, a blueprint for the renaissance of the capital as "a metropolis of social and ecological harmony" with "beautiful buildings, tree-lined avenues and new parks, where the commonest sounds are voices, footsteps and the buzz of the electric tram …".[1]

In the summer of the same year, the Architecture Foundation, a body that Richard Rogers chaired (and had been instrumental in founding), organized an exhibition at the Royal Exchange, at the heart of the City of London, that documented the City's recent architectural achievements.[2] In 1986 the deregulation of share trading, a key Thatcherite move alongside the abolition of exchange controls and a pro-enterprise tax regime, had ushered in the 'Big Bang', a huge expansion in financial services. London's global role in this area was given a dramatic boost, and banks, British and foreign, needed buildings capable of housing the new dealing spaces in which electronic trading in currencies and shares could be conducted. By 1992 a recession was biting hard, yet it was reckoned that, by the end of the following year, half of all the office space in the City would have been rebuilt as a consequence of the Big Bang. Office construction from 1989 to 1990, the height of the Thatcher boom, had equalled the total for the previous decade. The *City Changes* exhibition was intended as a celebration of the success of the City authorities in accommodating big new office developments such as those at Broadgate/Bishopsgate (330,000 square metres of offices over and around the rebuilt Liverpool Street station) and Ludgate – another 'over the tracks' scheme totalling 76,000 square metres – while caring for the City's four-hundred-plus listed buildings and twenty-two conservation areas. Both Broadgate and Ludgate were promoted by Rosehaugh Stanhope, an alliance between developers Stuart Lipton and Godfrey Bradman that set the pace for the renewal of London's commercial building stock. Lipton and Bradman had studied the 'fast-track' construction methods that prevailed in the United States and they proceeded to apply them to solving London's increasingly desperate shortage of new-style office space. At Broadgate (where the first four phases were designed by London-based Arup Associates) and at Ludgate, Skidmore, Owings & Merrill, the most prominent of a series of American architectural practices that had opened London offices, applied skills learned in Manhattan and Chicago. The use of prefabricated parts and the application of novel construction management methods were key elements in a revolutionary (by British standards) approach to design and construction. The more leisurely approach pursued at Richard Rogers's Lloyd's of London – which took eight years (1978–86) to design and build – now seemed irrelevant, while the exquisite and painstaking reconstruction of Bracken House (the former *Financial Times* building) by Michael Hopkins & Partners was clearly a one-off, a matter of biting the bullet handed to the Japanese developer when the building was unexpectedly listed.

The City's reconstruction campaign, which focused on the replacement of supposedly obsolete post-war office buildings (which nobody loved), had, in fact, been only a partial success. Against the odds, triumphing over abysmally poor communications and the inherent conservatism of the financial sector, 'Docklands' – a term applied to a huge swathe of riverside between Tower Bridge and the Thames Barrier – had managed to invade the traditional preserves of the 'Square Mile'. Canary Wharf had originally been conceived by American developer G. Ware Travelstead, who commissioned Skidmore, Owings & Merrill to draw up a 1985 masterplan for a huge new office city on the site of the redundant West India Docks. From 1987 onwards, Travelstead's successor, Olympia & York (which had developed New York's World Financial Center), realized the vision, capitalizing on the financial and planning incentives offered by the London Docklands Development Corporation (established in 1981 to regenerate the abandoned docks). With architecture predominantly by Americans (Skidmore, Owings & Merrill, Kohn Pedersen Fox and Cesar Pelli, who was responsible for the landmark, stainless steel-clad 1 Canada Square tower), Canary Wharf was hard hit by the recession of the 1990s, but by the end of the century was a huge commercial success, with up to 60,000 office workers based there and two new 93,000-square-metre towers flanking Pelli's 1980s icon, one of them designed by Pelli, the other by Foster & Partners.

For some critics, Canary Wharf epitomized the failings of Thatcher's London – "a symbol of 1980s smash-and-grab culture" was the verdict of Samantha Hardingham in her

Above
The Broadgate development spearheaded the redevelopment of the City in the later 1980s

Opposite
Richard Rogers's Lloyd's of London, completed in 1986, remains one of London's most striking modern monuments

sharply focused guide to London architecture.[3] Rogers and Fisher, surprisingly, praised its "solid and serious attention to urban design". The neatly maintained private spaces of Canary Wharf and Broadgate contrasted with the unkempt mess of the South Bank. Here was an area of London where the civic and commercial, idealistic and pragmatic, aspirations had confronted each other. It was here that they might profitably be reconciled, yet the history of the area was depressing. After the closure of the Festival of Britain, the Tory government had torn down everything on the festival site save for the Royal Festival Hall. (Ironically, the site for the festival had been created by demolishing streets of terraced houses that had survived wartime bombs.) The area between Waterloo station and Blackfriars Bridge fell into limbo. Richard Rogers's Coin Street project was subjected to planning inquiries in 1979 and 1981 and finally abandoned in the face of opposition from the Greater London Council. (The GLC, facing abolition by the Tory government, ceded its land holdings to a local community group, which began to build social housing there.) The GLC had been responsible for a major new cultural development on the South Bank in the 1960s, but when the Council was abolished, responsibility for this passed to a nominated board. Subsequent attempts (by Stuart Lipton, with Terry

Farrell, responsible for a previous scheme for the site commissioned by the South Bank Board, as architect) to use a degree of commercial development to fund upgrading of the declining South Bank arts centre foundered, while Richard Rogers's 'glass wave' for the South Bank, generated by a 1994 competition, was also widely opposed as an attempt to enclose and privatize public space. By the end of the century, a new masterplan by Rick Mather was in place, with a series of competitions proceeding for the design of individual components in the planned reconstruction. Meanwhile, Coin Street Community Builders, which had initially incurred critical censure for its unimaginative approach to new housing, changed its tune and commissioned schemes from Lifschutz Davidson and then Haworth Tompkins. But the debate over the South Bank continued – should it be developed to serve London, the world city, or maintained as an amenity for the small local population? The negative attitude of community activists in the area reflected an indifference to the needs of London as a whole.

The 1980s development boom produced much that was mediocre, characterless and transparently designed with a fast buck in mind. Yet it was also a period when a new generation of property developers came to the fore with a

The first phase of development at Canary Wharf was masterplanned and designed in the United States

Terry Farrell's Embankment Place was one
of the prime landmarks of the commercial
Post-modernist style

taste for distinctive architecture. They included Geoffrey
Wilson and Stuart Lipton, who had been Richard Rogers's
clients for the abortive Coin Street project on the South
Bank. Wilson commissioned Terry Farrell to design the
massive Embankment Place scheme above Charing Cross
station and was later part of the consortium that planned
the abortive Classical Revival redevelopment of Paternoster
Square. Lipton seemed omnipresent. Even as Broadgate got
under way in the City, he was starting work on Stockley
Park, the most celebrated of the new out-of-town business
parks that appealed particularly to the new technology-
based industries and to research-and-development
operations. The Stockley site was a former rubbish dump
close to Heathrow airport and the M4 motorway, on the
wealth-generating corridor out of London to the west. Arup
Associates were responsible for the masterplan for the site,
with buildings commissioned from Norman Foster, Skidmore,
Owings & Merrill, Ian Ritchie, Troughton McAslan and others
and set in lavish landscaping. Stockley Park became a
showpiece of new British architecture and was also a huge
commercial success, underlining Lipton's conviction that
good architecture represented a sound investment. In the
1960s developers had established relationships with 'safe'
commercial practitioners and stuck with them. The 1980s

saw developers launching high-profile design competitions
for prominent sites – Paternoster Square, Bracken House
and Stag Place, for example. Stag Place addressed the
future of a site close to Victoria station, where a Sixties
block owned by Land Securities was to be replaced. There
were submissions from the cream of the London
architectural scene, including Terry Farrell, Arup Associates,
Ahrends, Burton & Koralek, and Richard Rogers, but the
winner was Richard Horden. Horden, ironically, was later
dropped. (A revised version of his scheme by the EPR
practice was later built and is currently occupied by the
Department of the Environment, Transport and the Regions.)
His entry for another major competition staged by Land
Securities, for Grand Buildings on Trafalgar Square, was
also critically acclaimed, but was unplaced – Horden did
not achieve the success that many had predicted for him.

Back in 1964, when Ian Nairn pronounced London "one
of the best cities in the world for modern architecture", a
development boom comparable to that of the 1980s was well
under way: London had its first tall buildings, including the
Millbank Tower, New Zealand House, the Hilton and the Shell
Centre, and the post-war dominance of the public sector
was rapidly ebbing in the face of the Macmillan boom.[4] The
comprehensive redevelopment of areas such as the Elephant &

Castle, Notting Hill Gate and central Croydon was led by the private sector, with the planners colluding, as it seemed to critics of the process, in the destruction of London's physical and social fabric. Unashamedly 'commercial' architectural practices, such as those of Richard Seifert, Fitzroy Robinson and Gollins Melvin Ward, led the transformation of the City and West End. Seifert's most prominent work, the NatWest Tower (now Tower 42), was completed as late as 1979, to less than universal acclaim. Modern architecture seemed to have sold out to high finance. The anti-development, pro-conservation, pro-community mood that had derailed Rogers's Coin Street had been fuelled by the energy crisis of the 1970s. The identity of London was seen as under threat from developers and their architects. In 1984 the Prince of Wales's crusade for a more "humane" architecture was launched, with Ahrends Burton & Koralek's National Gallery project ("a monstrous carbuncle") and Peter Palumbo's Mansion House Square ("a glass stump", originally designed by the late Mies van der Rohe) singled out for particular condemnation. The style wars of the 1980s were under way. It was a war between two visions of London. The prince saw the aspects of London that he admired – Georgian terraces, City churches, green parks and squares – as the reflection of an orderly tradition of urban management inspired by a limited monarchy. Yet Wren and Nash were radicals in their day, as Richard Rogers pointed out. The prince seemed to have no comprehension of the real achievements of the Modern Movement or of the fervour for change that inspired the young architects of the Festival of Britain, Golden Lane and the Churchill Gardens estate and made them despise the stultified neo-Georgian of Sir Herbert Baker and Sir Reginald Blomfield.

The prince triumphed at the National Gallery (Ahrends Burton & Koralek fired, Robert Venturi subsequently hired) and at Mansion House Square (the Mies tower dropped), and his taste underlay the choice of Sidell Gibson for the redevelopment of Grand Buildings on Trafalgar Square – "an attempt to create a building no one would notice", commented the *Architects' Journal*. At Canary Wharf he appeared to have succeeded in getting the height of the Pelli tower reduced – the architect later complained that the proportions had been spoiled, but the real culprit was the Civil Aviation Authority, concerned with the safety of approach routes to the new City Airport. The prince's influence gave an (unintentional) boost to the rise of Post-modernism, a manner rapidly taken up by the leading commercial practitioners such as Fitzroy Robinson,

Chapman Taylor and Building Design Partnership (BDP), but responsible for a string of genuinely memorable buildings by James Stirling, Terry Farrell, Piers Gough, Jeremy Dixon and John Outram. Stirling, widely acclaimed as the greatest British architect of the post-war era, finished only one building in London during his lifetime, the Clore Gallery extension to the Tate Gallery (completed in 1985), a work remarkable both for its subtle contextualism and for its dynamic internal spaces. (Of the many unbuilt schemes by Stirling submitted for major London sites during the 1980s, the most remarkable was that for the National Gallery, a forceful response to history and place). For Charles Jencks, the Clore was one of the "canonic" Post-modern buildings of London, of which the real pioneer was Jeremy Dixon's St Mark's Road housing of 1976–79. For Jencks, writing in 1991 (as the London development machine ran out of steam), Post-modernism was "the modernisation of Modernism", a way towards a modern architecture both practical and popular. "Post Modern London means a diverse and contradictory city", Jencks wrote.[5] Post-modernism, Jencks argued, had effectively forged a new "London School" of architecture. Certainly, whatever its absurdities, it fuelled a new pluralism and, it might be argued, a willingness to countenance alternatives to the modernism that had ruled unchallenged since 1945 and produced much that was grim and, to use a favourite adjective of the Prince of Wales, inhuman. Though turned into a tedious parody of itself in the wrong hands, Post-modernism possibly opened the way to an acceptance of an expressive new modern architecture of form and colour during the 1990s and finally buried the myth of functionalism. It was no accident, for example, that Andreas Papadakis of *Architectural Design*, for a decade or so the most influential opinion-former on the London scene (he published the first monographs on Richard Rogers, Quinlan Terry and Will Alsop), moved on from promoting Post-modernism to launching deconstructivist architecture in Britain. (For the old moderns of the RIBA establishment, the two were equally suspect – deviations from the true gospel – and London was slow to recognize innovative talents generated by its own schools.)

The literal classicism that the prince championed had few takers among developers, despite the success, in a suburban context, of Quinlan Terry's Richmond Riverside. While able to secure the abandonment of schemes by Arup Associates and Richard Rogers for Paternoster Square, an area of obsolescent 1960s offices north of St Paul's

Norman Foster's Sackler Galleries at the
Royal Academy, completed in 1991, was
hailed as a masterly fusion of old and new

Cathedral, the prince saw his own favoured project for the area, launched by classicist John Simpson, shelved; a low-voltage, but basically modern, masterplan by William Whitfield was subsequently adopted. At Spitalfields, on the eastern edge of the City, classically inspired development proposals by Quinlan Terry and Leon Krier fell flat, while John Simpson's Venetian-style pastiche at London Bridge City was equally still-born. (A design competition for the latter development had produced an outrageously camp Gothic proposal by Philip Johnson, a shameless paraphrase of the Palace of Westminster.) A pompous neo-Georgian masterplan for rebuilding the government office quarter at Marsham Street was jettisoned under New Labour.

Some of these schemes were victims not of changing tastes but of economic realities. The 1990s recession saw sites at London Bridge City II, Spitalfields, the King's Cross goods yard (where Norman Foster had won a 1987 masterplanning competition), the Paddington Basin, Battersea Power Station, Paternoster Square and the South Bank all shelved, pending better times. "The party's over", commented the *Architects' Journal.* Canary Wharf developer Olympia & York was forced to call in the receivers. Among City schemes placed on ice were those by Richard Rogers for Daiwa on Wood Street and by Norman Foster for a site close by on London Wall, though Foster – who had built little in London – completed his Sackler Galleries at the Royal Academy in 1991, setting a benchmark for 'new–old' juxtapositions.

The (temporary, as it turned out) demise of Olympia & York in 1992 was sparked by the company's inability to make an agreed payment of £40,000,000 towards the construction of London Underground's Jubilee line extension, which was seen as the catalyst that would finally release Canary Wharf's real potential. The next year, however, John Major's government gave the go-ahead to this monumental project, completed seven years later. With Roland Paoletti as impresario, the project renewed the idea (generated by Charles Holden and Frank Pick between the wars) of the Underground as a patron of progressive architecture. With contributions by Michael Hopkins, Ian Ritchie, Troughton McAslan, Chris Wilkinson and Norman Foster, the Jubilee line extension looked set to be a showcase of the dominant high-tech tradition, soon to re-emerge on the commercial scene. But commissions to Richard MacCormac, a refined Post-modernist, van Heyningen & Haward and Will Alsop, a genuine original who belonged in no established school of design, underlined Paoletti's determination to produce buildings that responded to the variety of London itself and to eschew the uniform aesthetic approach favoured by Pick. The Jubilee line extension, completed behind schedule and over budget, nonetheless emerged as the most important exercise in architectural patronage in London since the Festival of Britain.

In spite of itself, it seemed, the Conservative government backed significant investments in London's infrastructure – Nicholas Grimshaw's Waterloo International Terminal was completed in 1993, though there was to be a long wait for the first Eurostar. New road links and the extension of the Docklands Light Railway improved the prospects for Docklands and opened the way for the development of the Royal Docks, the largest and most remote of the dock complexes (and the last to close). Margaret Thatcher's campaign against the welfare state had a huge impact on the housing, health and education sectors, but by the mid-1990s practices such as Avanti Architects and Penoyre & Prasad were producing distinguished social service architecture in the tradition of Lubetkin, Lasdun and Edward Cullinan, while new approaches to housing, pioneered, for example, by Dickon Robinson at the Peabody Trust, began to fill the gap left by the decline of the public rented sector. "While London drifts, Paris has tackled its problems with enterprise, even daring", argued Rogers and Fisher.[5] Paris had its *grands projets,* yet London's equivalents were to come, the product of the National Lottery that the Major government launched in 1994. The perception that London had suffered from the policies of the Tory years was, however, widespread. The abolition of the Greater London Council (GLC), which even Thatcher's greatest inspiration, Enoch Powell, had argued against, was seen as a vindictive and counter-productive move – the need for Londonwide co-ordination of transport and other infrastructure was argued by the City and by business interests. Unlike other Britons, Londoners generally backed higher spending on public transport and further restrictions on private car use – the Tories' transport policies helped lose them many seats around London, though New Labour was slow to begin remedying the critical problem of movement in the city and south-east region.

Towards the end of New Labour's first term, in fact, the government was locked in a destructive confrontation with London mayor Ken Livingstone over the future funding of the Underground that was resolved only after some very hard bargaining. Thameslink 2000, providing a frequent mainline rail service between north and south London and parts

Nicholas Grimshaw's International Terminal at Waterloo was a pioneering landmark of the new railway age, built to handle Channel Tunnel trains

beyond, looked set to go ahead, with three major new stations, and the long-awaited east–west CrossRail link finally got the green light (though it will take ten years to build). A decision seemed imminent on plans for a fifth terminal at Heathrow Airport, a project won in competition by Richard Rogers Partnership in 1989 – the scheme, the subject of a record-length planning inquiry, had been strongly opposed by west London communities, but was widely seen as inevitable. As much could not be said of the high-speed Channel Tunnel Rail Link, planned to carve its way through Kent and terminate, inexplicably, at King's Cross – with marginal gains for travellers content to use the more central terminal at Waterloo. Yet the project won determined backing from the government, intent on reviving the regeneration agenda for the King's Cross area contained in Foster's abandoned project for the goods yard.

When London surfaced from recession in the mid-1990s much of the baggage of the recent past had vanished. The Prince of Wales's influence had decisively waned – his decision to rename his Institute of Architecture and move it (in 2000) from Regent's Park to a converted warehouse in Shoreditch was symptomatic of new thinking in princely

circles. The Classical Revival was back where it started, in the world of country houses and estate villages – though Quinlan Terry quietly got on with a substantial commercial development in Baker Street. Traditionalist architecture was left to wealthy enthusiasts such as Christopher Moran (who brought in architects Carden & Godfrey and a team of experienced craftsmen to create a convincing neo-Tudor mansion around Crosby Hall, an extraordinary medieval survival removed in the 1890s from the City to Chelsea) and director Sam Wanamaker who, against all the odds, built the new Globe Theatre with Theo Crosby as his architect. Even HM The Queen employed Michael Hopkins for the visitor centre at Buckingham Palace. Nobody would own up to being a Post-modernist. The POMO fashion evaporated even more quickly than it had arrived and many commercial practitioners dropped the sub-Stirling manner in favour of sub-Foster. Its legacy has yet to be dispassionately evaluated. If one project sums up the reforming urban ambitions of the Post-modernists it is Dixon:Jones's Royal Opera House, first conceived by Jeremy Dixon in the mid-1980s as a collage of contrasting elements, breaking down a cultural megastructure into what appears to be a random accretion of city buildings. While the Royal Opera House was being completed, however, its architects had moved on to a cooler and more rational approach, boldly expressed in their extension to the National Portrait Gallery. Stirling Wilford's Number 1 Poultry could be glibly dismissed as an instant period piece, especially since it was completed after James Stirling's premature death in 1992, but commands respect as an ingenious marriage of public and commercial space with genuine civic feeling. Meanwhile, Piers Gough of CZWG continued to build with wit – what other architect has as his best-known work a public convenience? – but failed to win the large public commissions to which he aspired, possibly because nobody would take him seriously. Richard MacCormac moved on from an over-preoccupation with

detail, reflected in some of his Oxbridge college schemes, to the noble spaces of Southwark station and the dramatic simplicity of the Wellcome Wing at the Science Museum, though his masterly project for Spitalfields was consigned to the bin. William Whitfield, a practitioner of an older generation whose confident 1960s additions to the late Victorian Institute of Chartered Accountants building in the City had been lavishly praised by Nikolaus Pevsner, was seen as the only architect capable of welding together modernist and traditional elements to make an acceptable masterplan for the long-disputed Paternoster Square site – Whitfield's Richmond House in Whitehall, with a façade in a sort of streamlined Tudor Gothic style, is one of the oddest London buildings of the post-war era.

Stirling Wilford's Number 1 Poultry was the outcome of a twenty-year campaign by Peter Palumbo to develop the site at the heart of the City

Without doubt the most idiosyncratic major London building of the 1990s was the new British Library at St Pancras, designed by Colin St John Wilson, a pupil and associate of Sir Leslie Martin (whom he succeeded as professor of architecture at Cambridge and with whom he won the original commission – in 1962 – to rehouse the library on a site south of the British Museum). A decade later the site at St Pancras, in a drab and crime-ridden quarter close to two rail terminals, was acquired, but Wilson's building was completed and occupied only in 1997. For the Prince of Wales, it resembled "an academy for secret policemen". For most architects and critics, the building was simply an irrelevance, for all the admirable heroism of its architect's struggle to see it built – its rehash of Aalto-esque and Wrightian themes and desperate urge to relate to the context of Gilbert Scott's Gothic Revival St Pancras Hotel found few echoes on the contemporary scene. It did not help that during the 1980s red brick and pitched roofs had become the staple vocabulary of suburban superstore design. Set back from the busy Euston Road behind a bleak paved square and externally inscrutable, the library does not look inviting. The interior is, however, admirable for the generosity of its public spaces and the high quality of its detailing – it would be hard to argue that Wilson's long struggle was in vain. In the age of the private finance initiative schemes promoted equally by the Tories and New Labour, it seemed unlikely that a public building of such obsessive quality would be commissioned again.

Rogers and Foster had famously prospered on overseas jobs during the 1970s and 1980s, with relatively little work in Britain. Foster had suffered the cancellation of two exceptional projects: the Hammersmith transport interchange of 1978, which would have turned a polluted backwater into a hub for the capital (the scheme was cancelled and Hammersmith sank further into the mire) and the BBC headquarters scheme of 1982, abandoned by an organization with grand ambitions but no real vision or sense of purpose. The Channel 4 building, completed in 1994, could be seen as a typical Rogers commission, tuned to the specific needs of an end-user, with more drive than the hapless BBC, and drawing on the vocabulary of Lloyd's. The redesigned project for the Daiwa site saw Rogers working with a design-and-build contract and a brief for speculative office space – to produce, against all the odds, one of the most distinctive of new City buildings. For Lloyd's Register, Rogers slotted a new, low-energy building into a constrained historic site at Fenchurch Street – only the City's crass insistence that an

unlisted building be retained, and the new development thus denied any street presence, marred this subtle exercise in balancing conservation and radical new design. The radical and exploratory instincts that have permeated Rogers's work over the last forty years emerged strongly at the Millennium Dome, a highly appropriate and economical – as well as spectacular – container for the Millennium Experience at the Greenwich Peninsula on which Rogers's partner Mike Davies worked with Buro Happold engineers. Other big names were involved in the design of the Dome's zones – Zaha Hadid, Branson Coates and Eva Jiricna included – but the demolition of the interior, months after the closure of the Experience, provided a strange echo of the events of 1951. Despite an attendance of twelve million, the project had been deemed a failure, and the government was anxious to erase its memory and dispose of the Dome. (At the time of writing, its fate remains uncertain.) Foster & Partners' emergence as a mainstream commercial architectural practice was all the more striking, with half a dozen City projects in hand by 2001. Foster's willingness to embrace quantity alongside quality was seen by some as a worrying trend – yet Foster trounced his critics with the exceptionally innovative designs for the Swiss Re Tower, designed to replace the ruins of the Baltic Exchange, wrecked by an IRA bomb, and given planning consent amid bitter controversy. More than Seifert in the 1960s or Farrell in the 1980s, Foster was omnipresent in the London of the millennium, dominating the world of civic and cultural, as well as commercial, design. Swiss Re, incorporating radical new ideas on servicing and the environment, has its roots in innovative projects such as Willis Faber and even the very early schemes done for Fred Olsen. In contrast, Foster's British Museum Great Court is both modern and monumental, taking its cue, perhaps, from I.M. Pei's work at the National Gallery in Washington, DC, and the Louvre. Swiss Re is significant not just for its memorable form, but for its progressive environmental agenda. The recession of the 1990s had done little, in the absence of legislation, to persuade British developers and architects of the necessity of a move towards 'green' buildings – a well-researched and entirely practical project such as Future Systems' Green Office was dismissed as an idealistic gesture. In this area of design, as in many others, London's outlook was closer to that of New York than Frankfurt. Only slowly did British attitudes to environmental design change.

The Mound Stand at Lord's cricket ground, designed by Foster's former partner Michael Hopkins, was a popular success in the 1980s, combining traditional and modern materials – brick, steel and PVC-coated fabric – to produce a building with a strong identity and sense of place. Here, as at Glyndebourne, Hopkins transformed the image of an old-established institution. (At Lord's, he was followed by Nicholas Grimshaw and Future Systems, which designed the Media Centre, one of the most potent images of modern London.) But Hopkins's greatest challenge came with the 1992 commission for an extension to the Palace of Westminster to house MPs' offices, committee rooms and other facilities for the House of Commons. The new building, subsequently named Portcullis House, forms a structurally integrated whole with the new Westminster Underground station that lies below it, but while the station is an awesome work of engineering, Portcullis House is a carefully considered exercise in contextual modernism. Creating a building with a strong identity of its own that neither defers to nor contends with Barry's magnificent Gothic complex was a huge challenge. Seen from the South Bank, or glimpsed from Marks Barfield's London Eye, the success of the scheme is clear, and, though the façades are perhaps

over-detailed, the sheer bravado of the skyline, with its boldly industrial chimneys, commands respect; only Hopkins, perhaps, could have produced this confident dialogue with history. But it is the glazed central court, with its finely crafted roof structure of concrete, steel and laminated timber, that is the spectacular heart of the building – sadly one that is largely inaccessible to the electorate. Hopkins's recasting of the face of modern architecture was based on a real dialogue with tradition, not in terms of style but of materials and technologies. His quest for a new way is widely misunderstood, most often as a compromise with historicism, whereas Hopkins's radicalism lies in his ability to get to the roots of tradition, which, as T.S. Eliot insisted, "cannot be inherited ... if you want it you must obtain it by great labour". Hopkins's labour continues.

Nicholas Grimshaw's stand at Lord's was one of a number of London buildings of the 1980s and 1990s by his practice, of which the most widely acclaimed was the Waterloo Terminal. Grimshaw's continued attachment to the machine aesthetic and his fascination with metallic

construction (and reluctance to embrace a wider palette of materials) may have limited his appeal to commercial and public clients. His supermarket in Camden Town was a trailblazer for better retail architecture, though some considered its austere vocabulary inappropriate for the function of the building. Yet at the end of the twentieth century, Grimshaw was working on a massive regeneration project for Paddington, a reconstruction of Battersea Power Station and a major extension to the Royal College of Art.

As Foster, Rogers, Hopkins and Grimshaw, all well into their sixties by the year 2000, reinforced their grip on the London scene, younger practices moved into the front rank. Among them were Wilkinson Eyre, largely on the basis of its work for the Jubilee line extension; Lifschutz Davidson and John McAslan, the most successful of the 1980s practices with roots in the Foster–Rogers circle; and Allies & Morrison, a practice with a feeling for history and a fastidious and refined approach, forged in the Cambridge tradition of Leslie Martin, which has won it work in a remarkable range of contexts. Rick Mather is an architect of an older generation whose London work up to the 1990s consisted largely of restaurants, shops and domestic interiors, plus a solitary office scheme in Docklands. In addition to his work as masterplanner for the South Bank, Mather has recently become identified with major refurbishments to leading museums, which include the National Maritime, Wallace Collection and – the most accomplished of this series of projects – Soane's much-imitated Dulwich Picture Gallery. Even more striking has been the advance of Will Alsop into the inner circle. Alsop's early projects, carried out in partnership with John Lyall, were modest but highly original – the low-cost reworking of Tottenham Hale station is a good example. North Greenwich station demonstrated his skill at creating memorable form and using colour to dramatize it. The Peckham Library applied this skill to civic ends – the library was one element in a new public space at the heart of the district. Its impact on Peckham was comparable to that of Owen Williams's Pioneer Health Centre seventy years earlier – Alsop caught the mood of the local community, with its longing for change and improvement. The Peckham Library was an appropriate choice for the RIBA's Stirling Prize at the end of 2000, since it symbolized the mood of renewal and regeneration in areas that had missed out on the commercial bonanza of the 1980s and reflected, in particular, the remarkable transformation of Southwark. Already heavily involved in infrastructural projects, including CrossRail and Thameslink 2000, Alsop has moved into the commercial field with office projects in Southwark and the City, the latter involving an operation of urban repair for a quarter devastated by insensate 1960s planning, though his inspirational proposals for the reconstruction of the BBC's landmark site at Portland Place proved too radical for the corporation.

Alsop's new prominence on the London scene contrasted with the marked absence of projects by other innovative figures of his generation such as David Chipperfield, Zaha Hadid and Nigel Coates, all of whom have made London their base for international careers. Though Branson Coates completed an extension to the Geffrye Museum in 1998, most of its work in London has taken the form of interiors, including important retail commissions. Chipperfield's most significant London commission to date is a fit-out at the Natural History Museum, though, like Hadid, he is involved in major foreign projects. The architectural culture of London is strong, rooted in a lively critical discourse and in architectural schools of global reputation. Hadid's career was one of many launched at the Architectural Association under the leadership of Alvin Boyarsky. Tony Fretton, another Architectural Association-bred talent, was another whose projects were lamentably under-built, though his Lisson Gallery is a miniature gem and his 2001 town house in Chelsea a remarkable and uncommon instance of a modern house located not in a suburban grove but on a historic central London street.

The neglect of talents of this magnitude does not reflect well on London, yet a score or more of outstanding young practices moved on during the 1990s from the shop fit-outs, bars, restaurants and small domestic commissions that are the mainstay of a rising generation to much more substantial jobs. They included Allford Hall Monaghan Morris, Buschow Henley, Cartwright Pickard, Harper Mackay, Haworth Tompkins, Proctor Matthews, Rivington Street Studio, Tim Ronalds, and Walters & Cohen, with the names of David Adjaye, Jo Hagan, Softroom, Shed 54, Wells Mackereth and Foreign Office Architects all well tipped for solid success in the coming decade.

London's architects thrived in the context of renewed economic growth from the mid-1990s onwards (though by 2001, rumours of recession leavened the mood of optimism). The new century was heralded by a move to build high. Apart from Foster's Swiss Re, plans for new office towers at Bishopsgate (Kohn Pedersen Fox), Fenchurch Street (Wilkinson Eyre), Paddington (Richard Rogers Partnership and Nicholas Grimshaw) and London Bridge (Broadway Malyan/Renzo Piano) were announced, with Marks Barfield,

Victoria Miro Gallery is one of several commercial art galleries to have moved around the turn of the millennium from relatively cramped premises in London's traditional art quarter around Bond Street to far loftier spaces in the East End, where former warehouses are regularly being converted for new uses

buoyed by the triumphant success of the London Eye, floating the idea of a mixed-use high-rise, with a strong element of rented housing, for a site as yet unspecified. Arup Associates designed a high-rise replacement for Plantation House in Fenchurch Street, a huge 1930s classical office scheme that was the subject of a £20,000,000 rehab completed in 1992 – seven years later, the whole building was flattened. By early 2001 the issue of high buildings had polarized opinion to a degree reminiscent of the 1980s – English Heritage, backed by a coalition of amenity groups, led the anti-tower lobby, arguing, against the evidence of recent history, that London should remain a low/medium rise conurbation. For Mayor Ken Livingstone, well-sited, high-quality towers were a symbol of the dynamic social and economic life of London. Livingstone's support provoked the government to adopt a generally negative line, despite the supportive stance of the Commission for Architecture and the Built Environment, CABE – the Blair government's replacement for the abolished Royal Fine Art Commission. Local authorities were divided: Westminster, Tory-controlled and supposedly pro-enterprise, dithered and sought to limit new buildings to a height of no more than 100 metres. The City, ever aware of the threat of Docklands and Europe, was more receptive, as were the inner-London boroughs, such as Southwark, for which regeneration and job creation were priorities.

London in the early twenty-first century is a city of *grands projets*, both completed (Tate Modern, the Great Court, the Royal Opera House, Somerset House) and forthcoming (the troubled Wembley Stadium, the National Athletics Stadium and Foster's World Squares for All). The oft-quoted contrast between "private affluence and public squalor" is less apparent than it was two decades back and public (albeit Lottery) money is renewing the capital's cultural infrastructure. Yet London's *petits projets* are equally significant in the continuing restructuring of the metropolis. The art world, for example, moved eastwards and southwards. Paxton Locher's Jerwood Space inhabits a radical reworking of a Victorian school in Southwark. Other galleries moved to Hoxton and Shoreditch. The former hydraulic power station close to the Thames at Wapping opened in autumn 2000 as a new visual and performing-arts centre with fit-out by Joshua Wright of Shed 54. Artists and craftspeople colonized the great undercroft of the former Bishopsgate goods station in Shoreditch, site for an abortive tower project of the 1980s (and possibly for a major office scheme of the 2000s). The Victoria Miro Gallery moved from Cork Street to Wharf Road, N1. The idea of reinhabiting and

redefining areas of the city was hardly a novelty – in the 1950s Notting Hill was a near-slum, Clerkenwell and Bankside industrial quarters – but the push into the former industrial fringes produced a real architectural challenge. Buschow Henley addressed the issue of reuse in their mixed-use development at Shepherdess Walk, Hackney, while Cartwright Pickard's housing at nearby Murray Grove sought a new contextual modern vocabulary while utilizing prefabricated components for speed and economy of construction. At the Greenwich Peninsula, within sight of the Dome, Proctor Matthews' housing for the Millennium Village, colourful and strongly articulated, blazed the regeneration trail amidst a sea of mud and dereliction – the project was an act of faith in what could one day be a vibrant new district. After twenty years, during which the social housing stock diminished by nearly a quarter, the rented sector is back, with new agencies (such as the Poplar Housing and Regeneration Community Association, responsible for 4000 dwellings in the East End, or the Stonebridge Housing Action Trust) replacing local authorities as landlords and voluntary associations and trusts (such as Peabody) playing a revitalized role and addressing the needs of a varied clientele badly served by traditional council housing. For the first time in decades, new schools and medical centres command attention as architecture; practices such as

Penoyre & Prasad and Avanti Architects have a notable record in this area, while Guy Greenfield's medical centre at Hammersmith is a striking landmark as well as an outstanding community amenity. New public open spaces, such as the extended and transformed Mile End Park, with its Green Bridge by Piers Gough, and Patel Taylor's Thames Barrier Park, the first entirely new park established in London since the Second World War, have provided a latter-day interpretation of the public park of the nineteenth century. Culture projects downsized after the spending splurge that followed the launch of the Lottery. English National Opera announced a sensible and respectful refurbishment scheme for the London Coliseum, abandoning ideas of a new opera house on another site. Tim Ronalds's forthcoming reconstruction of the Hackney Empire has the attraction of catering for a far from élitist East End audience. As the rather mixed record of the Royal Opera House since its £200,000,000 makeover suggests, costly buildings do not necessarily produce great performances.

London architecture today is, on the one hand, a reassertion of the continuity of the city, on the other, a manifesto for radical change. Some were critical of the preponderance of conversion and reuse schemes among London's millennium projects, yet the background was a long period in which historic buildings and areas were wantonly

The cardboard pavilion by Shigeru Ban Architects and Gumuchdjian Associates, planned for Kew Gardens, reflects new approaches to building technology and the environment

destroyed – the whole of the London Docks, for example, vanished in the 1970s. It was against this background that the journalist Marcus Binney and a group of friends formed SAVE Britain's Heritage in 1975 – European Architectural Heritage Year. SAVE had its roots in the movement to rescue threatened country houses, but soon became embroiled in London issues. Its influence was critical in the reprieves granted to Battersea Power Station and the old Billingsgate Market (subsequently converted to a dealing floor by Richard Rogers) and in the defeat of Peter Palumbo's Mansion House Square. SAVE worked with Terry Farrell, an architect with a sure feel for combining old and new, on an alternative scheme for Palumbo's site on Poultry, only to see it eventually razed for James Stirling's Number 1 Poultry.

SAVE and the other amenity bodies, including the fledgling Twentieth Century Society, informed a steady move towards the recognition of old buildings of quality as a resource. By 2000, applications to totally demolish listed buildings in London were rare. Increasingly architects have the task of adapting not just Georgian and Victorian buildings, but also those of twentieth-century heritage, to twenty-first-century needs. Denys Lasdun's Keeling House, designed with a working-class community of the 1950s in mind, has been reborn, after years of dereliction, as an oasis of chic living. Erno Goldfinger's iconic Trellick Tower in north Kensington became a fashionable address, and Alexander Fleming House, the Perret-inspired office scheme he designed at the Elephant & Castle, was reprieved from demolition and converted into apartments for affluent young City professionals. Paul Hamilton's Paddington maintenance depot is now the headquarters of a retail group. Even Highbury Stadium, if and when Arsenal Football Club moves to a new site, could be converted to housing. And Battersea Power Station, left beached and apparently doomed by the failure of a 1980s leisure project, may soon be brought to life as a spectacular auditorium.

At the same time, London architecture pushes constantly forward, generating not only new talents but new ideas on a scale that neither contemporary New York nor Tokyo can match. Wigglesworth & Till's Straw Bale House, 'green' but immensely stylish, Shigeru Ban Architects and Gumuchdjian Associate's pavilion of cardboard, planned for Kew Gardens, and David Adjaye's Elektra House represent new London architecture at the cutting edge. The talents of the future are making their mark, as ever, in bar fit-outs, flat conversions and house extensions – the kind of job that Rogers and Foster's Team 4 was agonizing over forty years ago. Finally, there is the conundrum of Daniel Libeskind's addition to the Victoria and Albert Museum; his 'Spiral', seen on the one hand as an extravagant irrelevance to an institution that cannot maintain the immense complex of buildings it already inhabits, and, on the other, as the key move that will transform the museum, potentially into an icon to rival Wright's Guggenheim. When this extraordinary scheme came to planning consent stage, a bitter aesthetic battle might have been predicted, yet the building was approved: there is a new openness to change and innovation in London that did not exist in the boom years of the 1980s. Mass-housing developers now routinely commission schemes that, a decade ago, would have seemed impossibly leading edge and unsaleable (even if they were to gain planning consent). Perhaps it is the shift towards the public domain and towards a balance between social and commercial gain that has made Londoners look at architecture and architects – and even developers – in a less cynical light. London is even now not the grandest of the world's capitals. As Ian Nairn wrote in 1964, "it does not make a display of its best things".[6] Ordinariness is steadily becoming a rare quality as the tide of growth and investment and the fame conferred by literature and films permeates even the more obscure parts of the capital – how long before Hugh Grant stars in a romantic drama set in Neasden or Catford? Yet London is increasingly a place where old and new architecture are welded into livable spaces, where history and modernity coexist and feed on each other. As such it has lessons to teach the world.

1   Richard Rogers (with Mark Fisher), *A New London,* London 1992, p. xliv.

2   See R. Burdett (ed.), *City Changes: Architecture in the City of London, 1985–95,* London 1992.

3   S. Hardingham, *London: A Guide to Recent Architecture,* 4th edn, London 1999, p. 310.

4   I. Nairn, *Modern Buildings in London,* London 1964, foreword.

5   C. Jencks (ed.), *Post Modern Triumphs in London*, Architectural Design Profile 91, London 1991, pp. 12–13: a remarkably well documented account of Post-modernism in London, with all the major projects illustrated.

6   Rogers (with Fisher), *op. cit.*, p. 51, note 1.

7   Nairn, *op. cit.*, foreword, note 4.

BERMONDSEY UNDERGROUND STATION
IAN RITCHIE ARCHITECTS

CANARY WHARF UNDERGROUND STATION
FOSTER & PARTNERS

ELEPHANT & CASTLE MASTERPLAN
FOSTER & PARTNERS AND OTHERS

FOOTBRIDGE, PLASHET SCHOOL
BIRDS PORTCHMOUTH RUSSUM

GREEN BRIDGE/MILE END PARK
CZWG ARCHITECTS/TIBBALDS TM2/COMMUNITY LAND USE

HUNGERFORD BRIDGE
LIFSCHUTZ DAVIDSON

LONDON BRIDGE STATION RECONSTRUCTION
T.P. BENNETT/WILKINSON EYRE

MILLENNIUM BRIDGE
FOSTER & PARTNERS

MILLENNIUM DOME
RICHARD ROGERS PARTNERSHIP/BURO HAPPOLD/IMAGINATION

NORTH GREENWICH STATION
ALSOP, LYALL & STORMER;
WITH TRANSPORT INTERCHANGE: FOSTER & PARTNERS

SOMERSET HOUSE
PETER INSKIP & PETER JENKINS; DONALD INSALL ASSOCIATES;
JEREMY DIXON:EDWARD JONES

SOUTH BANK MASTERPLAN
RICK MATHER ARCHITECTS

SOUTHWARK UNDERGROUND STATION
MacCORMAC JAMIESON PRICHARD

STRATFORD REGIONAL STATION
WILKINSON EYRE/TROUGHTON McASLAN

THAMES BARRIER PARK
PATEL TAYLOR ARCHITECTS/GROUP SIGNES/OVE ARUP & PARTNERS

THAMESLINK STATION, BLACKFRIARS; CROSSRAIL, PADDINGTON
ALSOP ARCHITECTS

WESTMINSTER UNDERGROUND STATION
MICHAEL HOPKINS & PARTNERS

WORLD SQUARES FOR ALL
FOSTER & PARTNERS

BERMONDSEY UNDERGROUND STATION
JAMAICA ROAD, SE1

IAN RITCHIE ARCHITECTS, 1990–2000

The Jubilee line extension project produced a number of stations – Canary Wharf, North Greenwich and Westminster included – that are major architectural landmarks set at key points on the route. Ian Ritchie's Bermondsey is rather different. It sits alongside the bleak, heavily trafficked Jamaica Road, serving an area of south-east London that is far from gentrified. Indeed, there were doubts as to the need for a station at this point – intensive political lobbying was necessary to quash the threat of cancellation.

The route of the Jubilee line extension from London Bridge to Bermondsey follows the line of the 878-arch viaduct that carries the 1836 London & Greenwich Railway, arguably the world's first rapid-transit system, into London Bridge.

Ian Ritchie, one of the first architects to be considered for a commission for the Jubilee line extension, took on the Bermondsey job in 1990. The brief was to provide a local station, the equivalent of Charles Holden's street-corner stations on the Northern line, with few frills. It was assumed that offices or a residential development might eventually be built over the station, but the demand for either would follow on from the opening of the extension. The site was complicated by its proximity to a major road and by waterlogged soil conditions (in the eighteenth century Bermondsey had been a spa).

The completed station is distinguished by its directness and calm logic. The sunlit booking hall is entered directly from the street. The escalators extend downwards at right angles to the platforms, with natural light flooding into the great concrete box sunk into the wet clay. (In a Holden station, the escalators would be contained within tubes and there would be no natural light.) The aesthetic of the station is formed by the contrast between rough and finely finished concrete – seen in the 'blades' that provide structural support for the box – and by the "jewellery", as Ritchie describes the fit-out, which includes blue-glass benches on the platforms.

Bermondsey builds on the Hong Kong model brought to London by Roland Paoletti and transforms it into a lightweight but robust balance of engineering and architecture. At Bermondsey, the promise of the Jubilee line extension as a force for regeneration is fully realized. Like the slum churches of the nineteenth century, this is a work of art done for a poor neighbourhood – one that is already benefiting from the dynamic impact of the Underground.

Above
Platform level, with the concrete structure powerfully expressed

Opposite
Ticket hall, brilliantly daylit with a clear route from the street

Platform, with blue-glass benches designed by the architects

CANARY WHARF UNDERGROUND STATION, E14

FOSTER & PARTNERS, 1990–2000

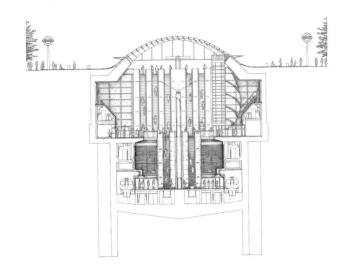

Canary Wharf station has the grandeur of a mainline rail terminal and the sleekness of an international airport, embodying all the expertise that Foster & Partners have developed in the design of public buildings and infrastructure over the last thirty years. Yet, for all its monumental grandeur, Canary Wharf is a link in the chain of the Jubilee line extension (Green Park to Stratford), one of a series of eleven new (or largely rebuilt) stations commissioned by the extension's architect-in-chief, Roland Paoletti.

Work on developing the Canary Wharf 'office city' began in 1987, and the buildings began to come on stream on the eve of the 1990s recession. By 1999, however, the project housed 25,000 workers – within a few years, this figure was to more than double. As existing transport connections, notably the Docklands Light Railway, were stretched to breaking point, the Jubilee line extension link arrived in the nick of time. The new station was designed to cope with future growth (40,000 passengers hourly) but could soon be working at capacity.

The site for the station was a former dock basin just south of Canada Square, the heart of Canary Wharf. A huge concrete box, 300 metres long, contained within diaphragm walls, was sunk into the drained dock and rooted into the waterlogged ground with deep piles. On top of the station box, a new park was created – a valuable amenity but also a vital practical device to prevent the station floating

upwards. If the engineering achievement involved in the project was heroic, it is the potency of the architectural expression, however, that places Canary Wharf firmly among Foster's major works (where his other recent works at Canary Wharf regrettably do not belong).

Externally the station has a discreet presence – the glazed entrance canopies are a development of those Foster designed for the Bilbao metro system. The experience of descending the banks of escalators into the 265-metre-long concourse is as memorable as any found in contemporary London architecture. Natural light floods into the space and there is a clear and direct route down to the platform level. Ticket offices and other service spaces are rigorously marshalled along the sides of the concourse and lighting and other services effortlessly integrated. The lightness of the architecture is astounding, considering the demands on the structure. Slim, elliptical columns support the roof, from which a mezzanine level is suspended. Architecture and engineering are, in the great Foster tradition, in complete harmony. One of the remarkable features of the Jubilee line extension is the variety of its stations – Southwark is complex and reflective, North Greenwich expansive and populist. Canary Wharf triumphs through sheer rationality – the inevitability of function expressed in noble form. The miseries of Camden Town or Tottenham Court Road seem part of another world.

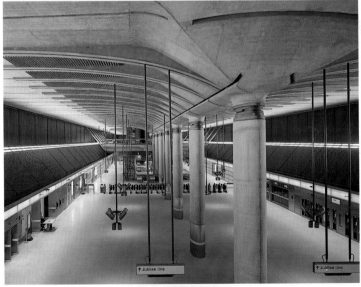

Above
Cross section, showing structure sunk into former dock

Station entrance, with glazed canopy illuminating the escalators

The station's majestic concourse level

Opposite
From the platform level there is a clear and daylit route towards the exit

West Plaza
Canary Wharf

ELEPHANT & CASTLE MASTERPLAN, SE1
FOSTER & PARTNERS AND OTHERS, 2000–2010

The Elephant & Castle was famously 'the Piccadilly Circus of South London', a lively district of shops, theatres and other places of entertainment. Wartime bombing and post-war redevelopment, carried out in the optimistic mood of that period, changed its character completely – and not for the better. The area is now dominated by roads, with pedestrians pushed to the margins, and by the large and undistinguished shopping centre. The station serving the Underground and Thameslink services is dismal and inconvenient. In short, nobody comes to the Elephant unless they have to.

Yet this remains the hub of South London, surprisingly close to the City and Westminster. The shortest route from Vauxhall to Tower Bridge is through the Elephant, and major cultural facilities like the Imperial War Museum, Oval cricket ground, South Bank Centre and Tate Modern are near at hand. The regeneration masterplan for the area is the centrepiece of Southwark's strategy for revitalizing the entire borough and is one of the largest projects of its kind in Europe. More than two hundred acres of land, including areas of post-war housing, are included in the study.

The plan seeks to give back the Elephant to the community by banishing traffic from the site. The largest public square in London – 200 by 85 metres – will be created as the centrepiece of the area, surrounded by shops, cafés and housing, with an open-air concert bowl and new arts centre. The new 1 million-square-foot shopping centre will be set below a seventeen-acre park. A new theatre, swimming pool, library and school are promised. The existing station will be rebuilt as an integrated transport interchange, serving the greatly intensified Thameslink system and providing for the Cross River Transit, the projected fast tram link from Kings Cross to Peckham and Stockwell. Major office developments are proposed over the railway tracks, with tall buildings as markers of change. The existing Heygate Estate, a conspicuous failure in social and environmental terms, will be demolished and replaced by new affordable housing.

This plan provides for a degree of change that, Docklands apart, London has not seen since the 1960s. The architecture looks promising and needs to be if the regeneration is to be, on this occasion, lasting.

Above
The Elephant & Castle masterplan aims to reinstate the area as the social, business and cultural focus of south London

FOOTBRIDGE, PLASHET SCHOOL
PLASHET ROAD, E13
BIRDS PORTCHMOUTH RUSSUM, 1998–2000

Half a million pounds' worth of highly practical engineering in the far East End has been transformed into a work of art by one of London's best (and most under-built) young practices. The school was originally two separate schools, one housed in an unremarkable building of the 1930s, the other in an extraordinary 1960s eight-storey tower by the maverick practice of McMorran & Whitby. About thirty years ago, the two merged – the problem was that they stood either side of a busy road. For decades, pupils had to dodge the traffic in all weathers to get from classroom to laboratory, from dining room to gymnasium. Municipal engineers finally came up with plans for a purely utilitarian steel bridge, with perspex panels tacked on as weather protection. Municipal planners saw the designs and promptly rejected them. Enter Birds Portchmouth Russum, a practice formed in the office of the late James Stirling.

The firm's 'reinterpretation' of the bridge proposals included giving the structure a twist, thus avoiding a mature tree previously threatened with felling. There was an idea of cladding it in stainless steel. This was ruled out on cost grounds, and the project stalled. It was revived on the basis of a strict budget, with structural input from engineer Matthew Wells. The structure is of standard steel sections, with a covering of lightweight Teflon fabric supported on steel hoops; the architects liken the effect to that of a Wild West wagon train. The fabric produces a luminous internal environment, but does not allow views out. These can be had from a viewing gallery, with seats, provided at a point midway in the 67-metre span.

Prefabricated off-site, except for the concrete foundations, the bridge was erected during the summer holidays of 2000. Its practical advantages are obvious, but it is also a striking and memorable object that has become a proud symbol for the school and a landmark in a mundane suburb.

Left
The boldly coloured bridge snakes across a busy road to provide a safe route between two school buildings

GREEN BRIDGE/MILE END PARK
MILE END ROAD, E3

CZWG ARCHITECTS/TIBBALDS TM2/COMMUNITY LAND USE
1995–2001

In comparison with other leading European cities, London has been slow to create new urban parks – in spite of the fact that the public park was pioneered in Britain. The Mile End Park is not entirely new. An open space was created here by the GLC in the aftermath of the wartime bombing that wrecked much of the surrounding area, leaving swathes of devastation. The 90-acre park extended south of Victoria Park towards the Thames, along the Grand Union Canal. It was an heroic effort, though the open space was seriously compromised and compartmented by roads and railways and by a local authority decision not to proceed with the demolition of an area of housing close to its heart. The initial

enthusiasm with which the scheme was implemented seems to have subsequently evaporated: in recent years, the landscape has been under-maintained, threadbare and, in places, unsavoury. A masterplan for, in effect, re-creating the park as a variegated landscape catering for the community and providing sports and play areas, quiet planted zones, an ecology park and areas for public art was published in 1995 after extensive public consultation. Supported by the local authority, business and community interests, it has been implemented over the last six years with funding from various sources, including the Millennium Commission. There are now seven distinct areas reflecting themes of

play, art, ecology, sport and fun, the whole being managed by an independent trust.

Mile End Road is virtually the midway point in the park's north–south run, a very busy traffic artery that needed to be bridged if the coherence of the landscape was to be maintained. A simple pedestrian bridge would hardly have addressed this issue. Instead, Piers Gough of CZWG had the idea of "mending" the hole in the park by building a planted link across the road. Gough was in some ways an obvious choice for this commission: his architecture is famed for its qualities of wit and accessibility, though, sadly, he has not won the major public jobs that he deserves. (Perhaps his most famous work is the

public lavatory/flower shop in Westbourne Grove, completed in 1993.) Constructed in 1998–2000, the 25-metre-wide Green Bridge reads as a natural continuation of the landscape – "you don't need to show people how it stands up", says Gough. "The point is the grass and trees, not the engineering." The bridge, carrying pedestrian and cycle routes, manages to be substantial and shapely, a piece of living urban sculpture. One drawback of wide bridges across roads – think of the typical Victorian railway bridge – is that they create dank and gloomy areas at street level. Gough addressed this issue by locating shops under the span, also providing valuable income for the new trust.

Opposite and below
The bridge is a vital link across the traffic-choked
Mile End Road, connecting two sections of a
linear urban park

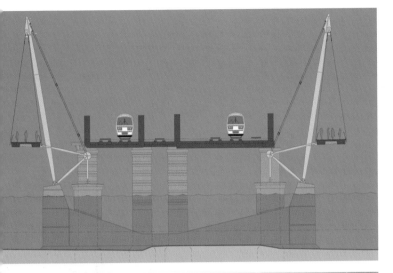

HUNGERFORD BRIDGE, WC2/SE1

LIFSCHUTZ DAVIDSON, 1996–2002

Hungerford Bridge is widely regarded as one of the worst eyesores in London – yet it seems destined to survive for many years to come. In 1986 Richard Rogers's visionary 'London as it could be' project proposed to remove the heavy and utilitarian Victorian railway bridge (which replaced an elegant suspension bridge by Brunel) and to replace it with a lightweight structure carrying a footbridge and monorail link, with the existing Charing Cross station closed. Terry Farrell's Embankment Place scheme subsequently cemented the station in place by covering the tracks with profitable office space, though the opening of the Jubilee line link to London Bridge and Waterloo makes Charing Cross an even more superfluous terminal.

Lifschutz Davidson's scheme, designed with structural engineers WSP and due to be completed in two phases in 2001–02, seeks to make the best use of the elephantine nineteenth-century structure, which carried a narrow pedestrian walkway on its eastern edge. Two new bridges are

attached to the existing bridge on its eastern and western flanks, so that, for the first time, pedestrians will be able to enjoy a view of Westminster from the Hungerford Bridge. The structural approach is as economical as that of the Victorians was cumbrous, and it evokes the spirit of Brunel and the 1951 Festival of Britain. (The project was generated by the ongoing campaign to revitalize the South Bank arts centre site and to improve its connections to central London.) The *in situ* concrete bridge decks are suspended on supporting steel rods from inclined 26.5-metre steel pylons sunk into the river bed. On the south side of the river, the bridge decks link directly to the terraces of the Royal Festival Hall.

Pragmatic rather than visionary, this project addresses a practical issue – that of encouraging people to cross to the South Bank – in a straightforward, but incisive fashion. But the issue of Charing Cross remains: one day it should be closed and the tracks across the Thames torn up.

Clockwise, from top left
Steel pylons located adjacent to the existing bridge caissons support the bridge deck from an array of fine steel rods

Typical bridge section at mid-span, showing the relationship of the new footbridges to the existing rail bridge

View looking towards Charing Cross station

View looking up river towards the Palace of Westminster

LONDON BRIDGE STATION RECONSTRUCTION

T.P. BENNETT/WILKINSON EYRE, 1998–2007

London Bridge, according to Sir John Betjeman (writing in 1972), "is, indeed, the most complicated, muddled and unwelcoming of all London termini ... . It seems to be several stations in one, and they are connected by toilsome footbridges and mysterious underground passages". In its present form, the station reflects many decades of underinvestment in the railway system. Badly bombed during the Second World War and subsequently patched and revamped in a random manner, Britain's fifth-busiest station, with 27,000,000 passengers passing through it annually (predicted to rise to 38,000,000 by 2010), provides an incongruous gateway to the City and the increasingly buoyant Borough quarter. Railtrack's proposals encompass total reconstruction: the result will be a station to stand alongside the best new transport buildings in France and Germany.

London Bridge, for all its inconvenience and squalor, is a railway site of huge historic interest. It was London's first station and the terminus of the line to Greenwich, which ranks as the world's first rapid-transit system, carried on 878 brick arches above the streets and alleys of south London. English Heritage's support for comprehensive redevelopment, including the demolition of a Grade II listed Victorian train shed, was therefore a bold move, but a necessary one.

Big changes at London Bridge were inevitable in the light of the Thameslink 2000 project. Terry Farrell produced plans for an intervention into the existing station that, though a major project in its own right, would not have addressed the basic problem of London Bridge: its accretive and disconnected character. T.P. Bennett was commissioned in 1998 to produce ideas for a more radical rebuild, and Wilkinson Eyre was later brought in to sharpen the designs. The current proposals reflect close collaboration between the practices.

The brief was hugely demanding: the station has to remain open throughout redevelopment and the site is tightly constricted.

Everything on top of the vast brick podium on which the station stands is to be demolished. An expansive new concourse will be carved through the undercroft from Tooley Street to St Thomas Street, with escalator links to the platforms above: the trains will be visible from the concourse. The new station interior will have a dramatic and expressive form, as can be clearly seen in the external elevations. The rebuilt London Bridge will be mainly a through station, with the terminal platforms reduced in number. A new bus station and better links to the Underground are envisaged, with new areas of the historic, still under-utilized, undercroft opened up for shopping and restaurant use. In line with government policy, a 70,000-square-metre office building is planned to straddle the rebuilt station and has been designed to provide a contrast to Renzo Piano's London Bridge Tower – a project that might be seen as inseparable from the London Bridge reconstruction. The offices will be accessed via a striking entrance pavilion on Tooley Street, a substantial building in its own right, conceived as an opportunity for a fusion of architecture and sculpture.

Approval of this project and of the London Bridge Tower would mark a shift in the balance of power and wealth in London, providing a major impetus for the cause of regeneration south of the river. It is not too far-fetched to imagine Borough and Southwark as major focuses of business and employment, with outstanding new architecture and refurbished historic streets forming a piquant counterpoint, and cultural and residential developments leavening the mix. Fingers crossed that neither an economic downturn nor the vagaries of the planning system derail this process.

MILLENNIUM BRIDGE, EC4/SE1

FOSTER & PARTNERS, 1996–2001

Norman Foster's victory in the competition for this new bridge, connecting St Paul's and the City with the new Tate Modern, seemed effortless, part of his sure hold on key London millennium projects. The Millennium Bridge project was developed in collaboration with Ove Arup & Partners and the eminent sculptor Sir Anthony Caro. The bridge was scheduled to open early in 2000, to service the new Tate. It did open – for a weekend – but was then closed (at the time of writing, probably until the end of 2001), to enable significant technical adjustments to be carried out to counter a pronounced wobble that occurred when large numbers of people crossed it on its inaugural weekend. Foster's detractors crowed and there was an element of *Schadenfreude* in some of the other criticisms made of the scheme.

Yet the problems of the bridge flowed from the high technical and aesthetic ambitions that underlay the project. This was to be the first new Thames crossing since the completion of Tower Bridge over a century ago and the first Thames bridge ever set aside purely for the use of pedestrians. The Thames is a big river, far wider as it runs through the City towards the sea than Dublin's Liffey or Paris's Seine. Foster's design capitalized on the thrill of being suspended high above the water, in the midst of a 320-metre span. The basic form is that of a suspension bridge, with two Y-shaped armatures supporting cables that run alongside the 4-metre wide aluminium deck, which is engaged by means of steel transverse arms. The cables rise no more than 2.3 metres above the deck, so that the effect is very different from that of the typical suspension bridge – Foster aimed at a thin ribbon of metal, a direct statement of the act of bridging the water. By night, the goal was to make the bridge a blade of light. By these means, those using the bridge were guaranteed uninterrupted views along the river, while the slenderness of the structure addressed the criticisms of those who feared that it would intrude into those precious views. In the quest of maximum structural economy, the design was finely tuned, perhaps too much so. Foster's daring may be vindicated when the bridge is finally brought into use.

Above
The bridge links the City and St Paul's Cathedral with the regenerated Bankside area around Tate Modern

Structural detail, with view up river towards Blackfriars

Opposite
The spare structure of the bridge has a sculptural elegance that contrasts with the solidity of Tate Modern

MILLENNIUM DOME
GREENWICH PENINSULA, SE10

RICHARD ROGERS PARTNERSHIP/BURO
HAPPOLD/IMAGINATION, 1996–2000

The Dome achieved more media coverage and generated more political and public debate than any British building of the last one hundred years. One needs to look back to the 1851 Crystal Palace to find a parallel. The Crystal Palace was widely derided and the 1951 Festival of Britain was disowned, and then demolished, by an incoming Tory government, yet both have gone down in history as successful ventures. In contrast, the Dome has been seen as something of a failure. At the time of writing its future remains uncertain – the zones and other internal elements that accounted for most of the total project cost of around £760,000,000 have been destroyed.

In itself, however, the Dome is a straightforward, low-cost (£40,000,000 for 80,000 square metres of space) structure ideally suited to the brief of accommodating large numbers of visitors (up to 35,000 a day were expected) and housing static exhibits and live events and with potential for continued use – the would-be users exist, if the political will exists to keep the Dome standing.

The origins of the Dome extend back into the early 1990s when the John Major government decided to set up the Millennium Commission as a recipient of

funds from the new National Lottery. In 1996 the former gasworks site at Greenwich was chosen as the site for the Millennium Festival with Imagination given the task of developing plans for the project. Richard Rogers, then working on a masterplan for the whole peninsula, was brought in to design the architectural setting. The idea of a masted, cable-stayed, fabric-covered structure was developed by Richard Rogers Partnership director Mike Davies, building on previous schemes by the practice, and engineers Buro Happold were enlisted to provide a structural agenda. Work began on site in summer 1997, and the Dome was ready for an official opening on New Year's Eve 1999.

With the zones (including structures by Branson Coates, Zaha Hadid and Eva Jiricna) stripped out, the Dome has once again become a grand empty space, served by a fine, and currently underused, transport interchange and a fast Underground link to central London. The structure is good for half a century and the fabric cladding should last twenty-five years: dismantling the Dome would represent a sad and wasteful end to the saga of the Millennium Experience.

Right
Interior view, showing the Talk Zone, now dismantled

The structure, seen here at night, has become a prominent East End landmark

Opposite
Detail, showing the masted, cable-stayed, fabric-covered structure and one of the brightly coloured service drums

Opposite
The industrial aesthetic of the service staircase contrasts with the backlit cobalt-blue glass wall behind

Below
The blue motif is continued in the mosaic applied to the wall surfaces and V-shaped columns

At platform level the underbelly of the passenger concourse is clearly visible

The integrated transport facility at North Greenwich was planned and commenced long before the emergence of plans for the Millennium Festival and Dome in 1996. Initially, the new station was intended to serve Port Greenwich, a huge residential and commercial development by British Gas of the former gasworks site on the Greenwich Peninsula, but the project fell victim to the 1990s recession and was never resurrected. The decision to proceed with the Jubilee line extension connection was fortuitous – it made the Dome possible and will serve as the hub for the future regeneration of the peninsula (which is already under way) and for public transport links to a wide swathe of south-east London and north Kent.

Will Alsop, then working with his former partner John Lyall, was approached in 1990 to develop proposals for one of the largest stations on the extension: the completed station is 358 metres long with three platforms. The practice developed the project with engineers Robert Benaim & Associates, with detailed design development and construction overseen by Roland Paoletti's in-house team. However, the station bears all the marks of Alsop's approach: colourful, strongly modelled, flamboyant and with a potent popular appeal – it is probably the Jubilee line extension station that has won the most plaudits from the travelling public.

The first idea was to build a station in an open cutting, surrounded by a green square and with the concourse suspended in the void. It would have been stunning, but the decision was made to give the station a lid. Construction began in 1995. The original concept was developed in the revised scheme, with the ticket hall becoming a great steel-clad 'boat' hanging in space, with views down to the platforms, which are accommodated within a spectacular train hall. The roof is supported on 21 pairs of 13-metre-high *in-situ* concrete columns in V formations, clad in blue mosaic. A huge wall of backlit cobalt blue glass provides intriguing reflections of escalators, people and trains.

The station has no expression at ground level. The logical course might have been to commission the surface-level bus station from the same architects, but it went to Norman Foster as late as 1996 and was built in little more than a year. Tony Hunt's structure cantilevers off column supports on the edge of the station, with the 6500-square-metre roof supported on steel 'trees'. The image is that of a great bird. Though Foster and Alsop have a very different approach, their respective contributions at North Greenwich work well together and the bus station, along with that at Canada Water designed by Eva Jiricna, represents a move towards civilizing travel conditions for London's long-suffering bus users.

SOMERSET HOUSE, STRAND, WC2

PETER INSKIP & PETER JENKINS; DONALD INSALL
ASSOCIATES; JEREMY DIXON:EDWARD JONES, 1996–2001

Like the British Museum's Great Court (see pp. 72–73), the ongoing Somerset House project is about turning underused, private spaces into a major extension of the public domain. London is a city where, beyond the green expanses of the Royal Parks, there are few oases of quiet away from the noise of the streets; the squares of the West End, for example, were traditionally private places. The project has also created impressive new spaces for the display of works of art, making Somerset House the nucleus of a new cultural and educational campus.

Somerset House was never strictly a public building. Sir William Chambers's monumental complex looks like a royal palace but was intended as offices for civil servants, with the fine rooms along the Strand frontage as accommodation for the newly constituted Royal Academy and Society of Antiquaries (which subsequently moved to Burlington House). There were no other grand interiors and the impressive central court and riverside terrace were used only by those who worked or (in the case of the Navy commissioners) lived in Somerset House. Chambers's grand plan was completed long after his death with the construction of new wings to the east (for King's College, which opened in 1829) and to the west (designed by Sir James Pennethorne in 1856 for the Inland Revenue).

London University's Courtauld Institute and Galleries moved to Somerset House in 1990, occupying the fine rooms and other spaces along the Strand frontage. The

Somerset House Trust was established in 1997 with the aim of gradually bringing the remainder of the site into public use as, potentially, London's Louvre. By the end of 2000, a series of major elements within the overall masterplan had been achieved. Inskip & Jenkins' galleries for the Gilbert Collection occupy the monumental spaces below the riverside terrace and part of the basement of the South Building and can be accessed *via* Chambers's Great Arch – once a water gate, but now beached on the Embankment – as well as from the Great Court. Inskip & Jenkins' design strategy combines careful restoration of the original structure with unequivocally contemporary interventions in a broadly high-tech manner. The economy of this approach provides an appropriate showcase for an extraordinary range of objects, ranging from the exquisite to the kitsch.

Donald Insall Associates' reworking of the Great Court included major below-ground works – lavatories are provided, for example, for large audiences attending open-air concerts – as well as the resurfacing of the court with setts, replacing institutional asphalt on what was a civil service car park. In the South Building, a restaurant, bar and shops have been provided as well as galleries displaying a rotating selection of works from St Petersburg's Hermitage Museum. Dixon:Jones' fountain, which forms the magical centrepiece of the Great Court, was commissioned in 1998, and its

choreographed battery of fifty-five water jets is a stunning invention, enjoyable and elegant. Less successful is the same firm's terrace café: its mannered woven acrylic canopies are flimsy on a windy spring day, and the bridge link between the riverside terrace and Waterloo Bridge shows little regard for the geometries of Giles Scott's bridge abutments.

The Inland Revenue continues to occupy the Pennethorne block and wings along the east and west sides of the Great Court, but the prospect is for a further retraction of civil service activities. King's College, in particular, is looking for expansion space as part of a development plan by Inskip & Jenkins. It took the determination of François Mitterand to banish the French foreign ministry from the Louvre: who has the clout to clear the tax inspectors out of Somerset House?

Above and opposite
The terrace café and the choreographed fountains in the Great Court are among the most striking interventions in this historic ensemble

SOUTH BANK MASTERPLAN, SE1
RICK MATHER ARCHITECTS, 1999–2007

The South Bank arts centre was created by the GLC in the 1960s on part of the Festival of Britain site around the surviving Royal Festival Hall. The festival had extended along the river from County Hall to Waterloo Bridge. The area upstream of the Hungerford railway bridge was subsequently laid out as Jubilee Gardens, with the land closest to the railway retained as a car park.

The GLC's last years saw an open-house policy applied to the South Bank – the Festival Hall was open all day, with events laid on to attract lunchtime visitors. With the abolition of the GLC and the creation of the South Bank Board to run the centre, plans for rejuvenating the site were commissioned from Terry Farrell. The idea was a public/private partnership with Stanhope developers. The arts facilities were to be enhanced with the help of funding raised from commercial development. Farrell's vision was of an area integrated into the 'real' London, with shops, bars and restaurants all approached at

ground level (most of the 1960s walkways were to be demolished) and the ethos of a cultural ghetto dispelled. The vision remained unrealized and the early-1990s recession left the site in limbo. In 1994 the South Bank Board, after an invited competition, appointed Richard Rogers to develop a new masterplan for the area based on the idea of a great 'glass wave'. This vision, too, proved illusory, and the scheme foundered when Lottery funders declined to stump up the sums required.

Rick Mather, already involved with revamping three major London museums, won the job of masterplanner for the South Bank in 1999, publishing draft proposals early in 2000. Mather's plan is more pragmatic than the Rogers 'wave' and less dependent on commercial funding than Farrell's developed masterplan of 1987. It takes as read the need to provide ground-level access to the buildings on the site, while proposing that the undercrofts of the 1960s Hayward Gallery/Queen Elizabeth Hall complex be 'inhabited' by shops,

galleries and new foyers. The trimming back of the 1960s walkway system will continue, though the Hayward is certainly to be retained and it is likely that the Queen Elizabeth Hall will also remain and be upgraded rather than demolished.

Mather seeks to make the Festival Hall a major focus of the site, with the restoration programme already begun – a separate commission – by Allies & Morrison being brought to completion. By removing service roads around the hall, Mather will give it an attractive landscaped setting, while a new block up against the Hungerford Bridge will allow shops and offices currently housed inside the building to be relocated, freeing up its spaces for public use. The circulation strategy aims to connect the South Bank more effectively to river crossings – Waterloo Bridge and the new Hungerford footbridge being designed by Lifschutz Davidson. A contentious element of the plans announced in 2000 was the inclusion of 'blade' office blocks at several points on the site, though more

generous public and charitable funding could remove the need for these.

The most striking new element in the Mather plan is the proposal to create a new raised park on the Jubilee Gardens/ Hungerford car park site. A new concert hall and new premises for the British Film Institute (to be relocated from its site below Waterloo Bridge) would be contained under the park, in what will be, in effect, a grass-roofed building rising to three storeys on the Belvedere Road side. A major attraction of the Mather proposals is that they can be implemented in phases over a number of years. Design competitions for individual elements of the masterplan are in progress. Given the long delays and the deteriorating environment of the South Bank Centre – in contrast to the ongoing transformation of Coin Street, Waterloo and the hinterland – it is to be hoped that a start can be made soon. Mather's plans are basically sound and achievable.

Opposite
The masterplan includes proposals for a raised park above new arts facilities, top, and the colonizing of previously disused undercrofts of the Hayward Gallery and the Queen Elizabeth Hall, bottom

Above
An overview of the site showing the new park

Right
Section drawing of the raised park that will replace Jubilee Gardens and Hungerford car park

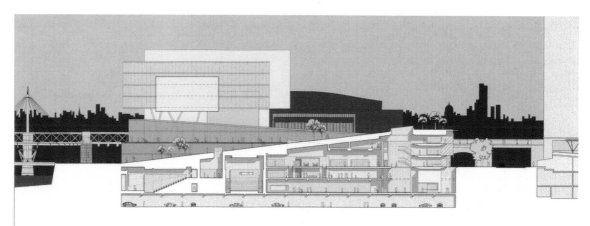

SOUTHWARK UNDERGROUND STATION
THE CUT, SE1

MacCORMAC JAMIESON PRICHARD, 1990–2000

The new Southwark station, incorporating a connection between the Jubilee line extension and suburban rail services at Waterloo East (previously a very badly connected, though heavily used, facility), produced what seemed initially a surprising commission. Richard MacCormac's approach to architecture, strongly contextual and rooted in history, is far removed from that of, say, Norman Foster, Ian Ritchie or Wilkinson Eyre, with none of the explicit concern for structural expression that tends to characterize their work. Nonetheless, the station is one of the delights of the Jubilee line extension and one of MacCormac's finest works to date.

It is no coincidence that this is the station serving Tate Modern, as its union of engineering and art is both subtle and appropriate. Like many earlier stations on the Underground, Southwark is located on a street corner amidst an established, downbeat urban scene. The exterior of the ticket hall is dignified, but unshowy, designed as the base of a forthcoming commercial development. The booking hall itself is a drum, relatively compressed in feel and evoking, consciously perhaps, Holden's Arnos Grove of the 1930s. The route from here to the platforms is, in MacCormac's vision, an "episodic journey". The passenger descends escalators to an intermediate concourse, a clearly subterranean space, but lofty in scale – 16

metres high – and filled with natural light from above. On one side, a heavy masonry wall contains the great 'scoops' of the escalator shafts down to the platforms. Balancing it is a curved wall made of 660 pieces of specially cut blue glass, a collaboration between MacCormac, engineers Tony Hunt and Adams Kara Taylor, and artist Alexander Beleschenko – the inspiration, it seems, was Schinkel's famous design for the Queen of the Night's castle in *The Magic Flute.* After the openness of this space, the escalator shafts are compressed, like those in a Holden station, leading to a lower concourse, a barrel-vaulted space lined in unpolished stainless steel from which the platform tunnels are entered.

The engineering challenge at Southwark was considerable, since the station sits under the Victorian viaduct of the railway into Charing Cross. An access tunnel from the intermediate concourse runs through to a new Waterloo East ticket hall, executed as a steel and glass shell wrapped around the viaduct. Not the least achievement of the Jubilee line extension project has been the closer integration of London's transport systems. Given the pace of development in the Bankside and Waterloo areas, the station is a vital new amenity – it seems amazing that it was once seriously proposed to delete it from the Jubilee line extension programme.

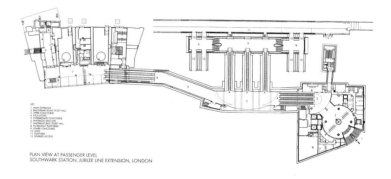

PLAN VIEW AT PASSENGER LEVEL
SOUTHWARK STATION, JUBILEE LINE EXTENSION, LONDON

Above
Plan showing the progression of spaces from the ticket hall, through the upper concourse, to the new Waterloo East concourse

Opposite, top left
At platform level the new Jubilee line stations reveal a unified aesthetic

Opposite, top right
Intermediate concourse, showing the curved wall of blue glass

Opposite, bottom
The vaulted space of the platform-level concourse is pierced by the dramatic staircase

STRATFORD REGIONAL STATION, E15

WILKINSON EYRE/TROUGHTON McASLAN, 1994–99

Stratford, the 'capital of the East End', is the end of the line for the Jubilee line extension. It has always been an important railway centre: the line from East Anglia into London passed through in the 1840s and a major railway works was developed there. Since the Second World War, the Central line has provided a link to the heart of London. A more recent arrival has been the Docklands Light Railway. The Cross Channel Rail Link, with Stratford a stop on the route from the Channel to St Pancras, will complete this concentration of rail links.

The new station at Stratford had to be far more than an Underground station. The opportunity was taken to improve and rationalize greatly the existing station, where mainline, Underground and North London line services and bus links were badly connected. Wilkinson Eyre created a two-level terminal, with the North London line services integrated into the building, which forms the public face to the entire transport complex. Jubilee line extension services

use surface platforms, with attached staff accommodation in rigorously rational style, designed by Troughton McAslan.

Wilkinson Eyre's great glazed concourse, with a sheer glass façade addressing the town centre, is a virtuoso exercise in terms of its structural economy, thanks to engineers Ove Arup, and innovative use of glazing. The south-facing street front is angled to avoid solar gain and glare. The double skin of the roof is designed to act as a thermal generator, drawing warm air out of the building. The building, which looks like a high-profile air terminal, works wonders for the battered image of public transport.

Wilkinson Eyre was also responsible for the Jubilee line extension's servicing depot at Stratford, designed and built in 1991–96. With all the grandeur of a Victorian train shed, the depot is the operational and spiritual heart of the Jubilee line extension. Sadly, it is completely inaccessible to the public.

Right
The station, with its elegantly sweeping form, serves as a transport hub for the East End and a focal point for Stratford town centre

Opposite
The lofty hall of the station contrasts with the functional rigour of the new Jubilee line platforms

THAMES BARRIER PARK
NORTH WOOLWICH ROAD, E16
PATEL TAYLOR ARCHITECTS/GROUP SIGNES/
OVE ARUP & PARTNERS, 1995–2000

The Thames Barrier, 520 metres in width and opened in 1982, could be reckoned the GLC's greatest gift to London as rising tides pose an increasing threat to wide swathes of the capital. The idea of a really large public park – half the size of St James's Park – adjacent to the northern end of the Barrier, on derelict land heavily polluted by industry, was one of the last projects of the London Docklands Development Corporation and was intended as a contribution to the regeneration of the Silvertown area and the Royal Docks. A design competition that elicited over 200 entries was held in 1995, and two schemes, this one and a rival proposal by Kathryn Gustafson/Peter Clash, were shortlisted. The Patel Taylor scheme was implemented in 1997–2000.

The competition brief had referred to "the metropolitan promise of the site as well as the recreational needs of the local population". This was to be a space for all London, not just for East Enders. It was

Patel Taylor's response that won them the job. They proposed a park of five distinct areas or "settings": the Plateau, with its views over the river; the Green Dock, a cutting through this space heavily planted and crossed by bridges, a quiet place for thinking and relaxing; the River Promenade; the Peripheries, with tracks for walkers, runners and cyclists; and a series of play areas set aside for team games and for children. The design of the park is thoroughly architectural, with a strong and legible plan, and its realization in tough and appropriate materials is entirely in keeping with the character of Docklands.

The park is an excellent amenity in its own right, and it was ironic that Ken Livingstone, former leader of the GLC and newly elected Mayor of London, came to open it late in 2000. It has also generated a great deal of development in the surrounding area, with scrapyards and oil depots giving way to houses, schools and shops.

Opposite and above
The park is heavily architectural and provides a variety of spaces, including a memorial, opposite, top right, to the East Enders who were killed in the Second World War

THAMESLINK STATION, BLACKFRIARS, EC4
CROSSRAIL, PADDINGTON, W2

ALSOP ARCHITECTS, 1993–

Will Alsop was commissioned to design the CrossRail station at Paddington in 1993 and the Thameslink station at Blackfriars two years later. Both projects, linking east and west and north and south London respectively, await a final go-ahead, following long planning and funding delays, but both are fundamental to the expanded public transport system seen as vital to London's continuing prosperity. A broad agreement to proceed with CrossRail was given by the government in spring 2001, but construction could take a decade.

Paddington is CrossRail's point of arrival in central London, where it enters a tunnel extending beyond Liverpool Street in the east. The site for the new station is in Eastbourne Terrace, west of Brunel's great terminus. The entire street will be excavated to form a deep trench in which the station sits, and connections into it have already been constructed as part of Nicholas Grimshaw's ongoing reconstruction of the mainline station. The CrossRail proposals build on the lessons of Alsop's outstanding Jubilee line station at North Greenwich. The great void of the station is naturally illuminated from a light beam cut into the road above, covered by a lightweight glazed canopy at street level. From here the escalators cascade down through a hugely dramatic space defined by the columns and cross-braces that support the structure. Colour will be used with Alsop's customary boldness. North Greenwich is stunning, but

Paddington could be a masterpiece on a grand scale. Given the utilitarian approach being promoted for the design of new transport facilities in London – ignoring the huge success of the Jubilee line – one hopes that Alsop's inspirational scheme will be implemented and not watered down by Private Funding Initiative or contract management procedures. (Brunel, thank God, never had to work under the yoke of Gordon Brown's Treasury.)

Blackfriars has been a focus of attention for Alsop for some years. He is currently developing proposals for Puddle Dock on the north end of Blackfriars Bridge and in 1996 produced a striking scheme (since abandoned) for new premises for the Institute of Contemporary Arts, using the piers of the demolished London, Chatham & Dover railway bridge. Alsop's station for Thameslink 2000 (as it optimistically used to be known) occupies the span of the surviving rail bridge across the Thames, with entrances to north and south. The station is yards from Tate Modern in an area where new office developments by Norman Foster and Lifschutz Davidson are in the pipeline. The original proposals wrapped the platforms in a mesh of glazing, lightly carried on a spectacular steel frame. There were objections to the impact of this on river views and a more conventional, though highly elegant, series of platform canopies and wind screens is now proposed.

Above
The new CrossRail station at Paddington will be set in a deep trench, expressed at surface level by a striking glazed fin that allows daylight to penetrate down to platform level

Opposite
The Thameslink station at Blackfriars straddles the existing railway bridge across the River Thames, while the existing station will be redeveloped as a commercial space

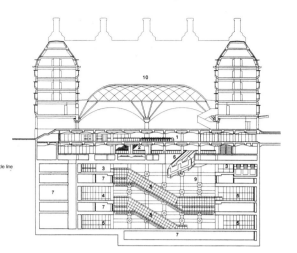

10m

WESTMINSTER UNDERGROUND STATION, SW1

MICHAEL HOPKINS & PARTNERS, 1991–2000

At first sight, the monumentally austere interior of Westminster station, completely rebuilt as part of the Jubilee line extension project, might appear to have little in common with Michael Hopkins's beautifully crafted Portcullis House (see pp. 212–13), of which it forms a vast undercroft. Yet the two projects were designed and built in tandem and are structurally indivisible.

An interchange with the District line at Westminster was planned for the extension project from the beginning. The existing station was part of London's first underground railway, opened in the 1860s, and had to be accommodated (and kept open) as the 40-metre-deep box for the extension was excavated around it. The proximity of Big Ben – a street's width away from one of the biggest holes in London – further complicated the engineering of the station.

Lowering the level of the District line tracks by 300 millimetres – no mean operation in itself – secured headroom for a new booking hall a level below the central courtyard of Portcullis House. The District line is one level below. The Jubilee line extension is accessed *via* banks of escalators (seventeen in total) threading through the main structural columns, with the deep platforms stacked one above the other outside the edge of the station box.

The predominant impression of the station is one of constant movement. Trimmings are kept to a minimum: the aesthetic is formed by the raw materials of the structure: rough and polished concrete, and stainless steel. Architecture and engineering come together in a fine balance, fulfilling an ambition that lay at the very centre of the Jubilee line extension project.

Opposite
The banks of escalators set amid the steel-and-concrete structure of the deep station activate one of the most exciting spaces on the new Jubilee line

Left
East–west section, demonstrating how the station provides the structure of Portcullis House above (see pp. 212–13)

District and Circle line platforms, which had to be accommodated between the Jubilee line platforms below and Portcullis House above

Jubilee line platform, with its distinctive steel panels and the glazed safety screen that is common throughout the Jubilee line extension

WORLD SQUARES FOR ALL

FOSTER & PARTNERS, 1997–

The idea of rescuing key areas of central London from domination by road traffic and creating pedestrian-friendly spaces was strongly promoted by Richard Rogers in his 'London as it could be' project of 1986 and in his subsequent campaigns. It was ironic, therefore, that it was Norman Foster, rather than Rogers, who was selected in 1997 to bring the vision to a degree of reality. Promoted by Westminster Council in conjunction with central government, World Squares for All focused on both Trafalgar Square and Parliament Square, both of which feature public spaces islanded by busy roads. Foster's radical proposals proved controversial, since it was suggested that curbing traffic in these locations would create traffic jams elsewhere and damage the commercial life of the capital. Tourism is, in fact, one of the major generators of wealth and employment in the West End, and the project addressed the setting of such key

monuments as the National Gallery, Westminster Abbey and the Palace of Westminster. Westminster Council, however, steadily backtracked on its commitment to the project, which seemed to drift into limbo.

A major boost to World Squares for All came with the election of Ken Livingstone as London mayor in 2000. There is now the prospect of a start on the Trafalgar Square remodelling scheme, with the road that separates the square from the National Gallery removed and pedestrians finally allowed to flow freely between the two. The proposals for Parliament Square received a setback after the riots of May Day 2000, with fears that greater pedestrianization might provide a focus for demonstrations.

Despite the splendours of its royal parks, London continues to have a far smaller area of traffic-free spaces in its built-up core than any other major European city, while many of the capital's squares are barred to the public.

MUSEUMS AND GALLERIES

DULWICH PICTURE GALLERY
RICK MATHER ARCHITECTS

MUSEUM OF FASHION AND TEXTILES
RICARDO LEGORRETA/ALAN CAMP ARCHITECTS

NATIONAL MARITIME MUSEUM
RICK MATHER ARCHITECTS

NATIONAL PORTRAIT GALLERY EXTENSION (ONDAATJE WING)
JEREMY DIXON:EDWARD JONES

THE QUEEN ELIZABETH II GREAT COURT, THE BRITISH MUSEUM
FOSTER & PARTNERS

TATE BRITAIN
JOHN MILLER & PARTNERS

TATE MODERN
HERZOG & DE MEURON

VICTORIA AND ALBERT MUSEUM SPIRAL
DANIEL LIBESKIND/OVE ARUP & PARTNERS

THE WALLACE COLLECTION
RICK MATHER ARCHITECTS

WELLCOME WING, THE SCIENCE MUSEUM
MacCORMAC JAMIESON PRICHARD

DULWICH PICTURE GALLERY, SE21
RICK MATHER ARCHITECTS, 1996–2000

For John Summerson, Dulwich Picture Gallery was not only "one of [Sir John] Soane's most able and revealing designs", but also a building that "as a whole reaches a level of emotional eloquence and technical performance rare in English, or indeed in European architecture". The gallery was constructed in 1811–14 under the terms of the will of the late Sir Francis Bourgeois (1757–1811), to house his remains and those of the great collector Noel Desenfans, who had died a few years earlier, leaving a collection of 370 pictures that went to Dulwich. The combination of mausoleum and art gallery was uncommon, the site, hard against the old buildings of Dulwich College to the north, awkward: Soane envisaged the building as one side of a quadrangle, but this was never realized. There were several minor extensions, and a certain amount of internal rearrangement, during the first half of the twentieth century. During the Second World War, the gallery was severely damaged by bombing in 1940 and 1944 and was rebuilt, to a tight budget, in 1950–52.

By the 1970s the gallery was a rather forlorn place, with serious funding problems and still run by the college. Giles Waterfield's directorship saw major changes: independent trustees took over, the building was made more attractive, with Soanean colours partly restored inside, and visitor numbers doubled; the educational activities of the gallery, in particular, blossomed. Rick Mather's millennium project, combining refurbishment and restoration of Soane's hugely admired and widely emulated gallery and the construction of a major extension to provide storage, offices and visitor and custom-made education facilities, was the culmination of this process of recovery and is the most successful of Mather's three major London museum projects of this period.

Any addition to an iconic monument of this order was bound to be controversial. An ideas competition of the early 1990s – there was no funding – proposed an extension to the south of Soane's building. Mather was the winner of a limited competition in 1996. The success of his scheme, funded by Lottery money and private donations, lies in its lightness of touch and its emphasis on redefining the important garden setting of the gallery and connecting it to the village street beyond. The new development provides a cloister that links the Old College with the gallery and provides space for new and relocated activities, freeing up Soane's interiors for the display of works of art. The gallery itself was carefully restored, with original decorative schemes and finishes reinstated and new environmental and security systems installed.

Above
The original galleries by Sir John Soane have been conscientiously refurbished

Opposite
The new cloister links the existing buildings, and provides office and education spaces and a café

MUSEUM OF FASHION AND TEXTILES
BERMONDSEY STREET, SE1

RICARDO LEGORRETA/ALAN CAMP ARCHITECTS, 1995–2003

This is Ricardo Legorreta's only European project so far, though he is currently working on a hotel in Bilbao. The idea of commissioning the Mexican master was fashion designer Zandra Rhodes's – he had built a house for a friend of hers in California. Surprisingly, perhaps, Southwark planners and the local community liked his ideas and welcomed Rhodes's vision of creating a personal museum for her collection – like Paxton Locher's Jerwood Space in nearby Union Street a spin-off of

the process of arts-based regeneration spreading out from Tate Modern. Not even the bright colours dimmed their enthusiasm and, after years of planning, work began, with local practice Alan Camp Architects collaborating with Legorreta.

The museum is scheduled to open "within a couple of years", the relaxed pace of the project reflecting Ms Rhodes's character. Part of Camp's task was to make the scheme commercially viable, and eight apartments were included, as well as a

restaurant (Rhodes has the penthouse).

The vivid colours applied to the development are typical of Legorreta but not of London; the combination of shocking pink with vivid orange is the antithesis of conventional 'good' taste. In the 1980s Post-modernists tried to achieve equally striking results but rarely, with the possible exception of Piers Gough, hit the right note. This development could be on the edge of downtown Los Angeles but looks good right where it is.

Below and opposite
The museum, with apartments above, forms an exotic addition to an otherwise gritty urban landscape

NATIONAL MARITIME MUSEUM GREENWICH, SE10

RICK MATHER ARCHITECTS, 1996–99

Rick Mather was brought into the National Maritime Museum project after a previous development project had been rejected for Lottery funding. The museum was established at Greenwich in the 1930s, inhabiting the long nineteenth-century wings built either side of Inigo Jones's famous Queen's House to contain the Royal Naval Asylum, a school for seamen's orphans. The result was a museum that extended in a straight line, east to west, with few really impressive spaces.

Mather took up the (fairly obvious) idea – part of the abandoned scheme – to roof over an open court, which had been merely wasted space in the western wing of the museum, and use it to contain large exhibits. But his new masterplan was effectively a reappraisal of the entire building, concentrating on establishing new connections between disparate

spaces. The most spectacular element in the scheme is the reconstructed Neptune Court, with what is claimed to be Europe's largest free-span glazed roof, designed with the assistance of Building Design Partnership (BDP) engineers. The roof covers a two-level public space: a raised square occupies the centre, with enclosed galleries, used for displaying light-sensitive materials, below. There are bridge links from this level to the first-floor museum galleries. The strategy ensures optimum use of space, but the visual impact of the glazed roof is inevitably reduced.

Mather's role at Greenwich has since expanded: he has designed a visitor centre, and is developing a masterplan, for the Royal Naval Hospital, now run by an independent trust and used for educational and cultural purposes.

Opposite and below
The central court, with its glazed roof and walls
either side of the existing stone pavilion, adds a
new dimension to the previously linear spaces
of the museum

NATIONAL PORTRAIT GALLERY EXTENSION (ONDAATJE WING), ST MARTIN'S PLACE, WC2

JEREMY DIXON:EDWARD JONES, 1994–2000

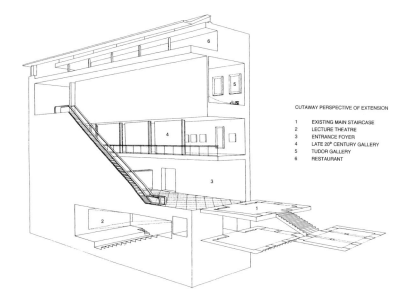

CUTAWAY PERSPECTIVE OF EXTENSION

1 EXISTING MAIN STAIRCASE
2 LECTURE THEATRE
3 ENTRANCE FOYER
4 LATE 20ᵗʰ CENTURY GALLERY
5 TUDOR GALLERY
6 RESTAURANT

Jeremy Dixon and Edward Jones, who formed their present partnership in 1989, have been identified in the past as Post-modernists – the Royal Opera House, on which Dixon began work as early as 1984, is essentially an urban collage. In contrast, the National Portrait Gallery millennium project is an exercise in minimalism, an ingenious and economical insertion into the tight fabric of the West End that has transformed the character of the gallery.

The original National Portrait Gallery building dates from 1896 and is the work of the church architect Ewan Christian, who squeezed it on to an awkward site behind the National Gallery (to which it appeared to form an addition). The interior suffered from its unavoidably vertical character – the Duveen Wing of the 1930s utilized the only space available for expansion. Many visitors never got as far as the top floor. Some – Ian Nairn, for example – loved the melancholy quiet of the place, but many Londoners never ventured inside. Dixon:Jones, appointed by director Charles Saumarez Smith and his trustees in 1994, broke the impasse in which the gallery was caught, proposing that a rear service yard, overlooked by National Gallery offices, be developed as a new central circulation space. In return for losing its rights of light, the National Gallery was ceded National Portrait Gallery space along St Martin's

Place. The new wing is slotted into the yard. A three-storey-high atrium contains an escalator that invites visitors to ascend to the top of the building and percolate downwards – at every level, the new wing is smoothly linked into the Christian building. (Some nifty adjustments to levels, with steps and mosaic floors seamlessly adapted, were required – there is, for the first time, total access for the disabled.) The structure is extremely economical – new twentieth-century galleries at first-floor level are suspended from above. A lecture theatre is provided at basement level.

The finishing touch to the transformation is provided by the new restaurant, a loggia that perches on top of the extension. It looks out across the domes, chimneys and skylights of William Wilkins's National Gallery – a miniature Classical landscape – to Nelson's Column, Whitehall and the Palace of Westminster. There was much agonizing over its design – planners feared it could intrude into views of the National Gallery. But its presence is elusive. Indeed, that term could be applied to the entire scheme: nothing seems to have changed at the National Portrait Gallery, until you get past the front door. The charm of the place has not been lost, but it has been intelligently equipped to deal with the demands of a new generation of visitors.

Top right
The extension is shoehorned into a former service yard of the gallery

Bottom right and opposite
The new wing, with its prominent three-storey escalator, links all levels of the nineteenth-century building, many of which were previously little visited

THE QUEEN ELIZABETH II GREAT COURT
THE BRITISH MUSEUM, WC1

FOSTER & PARTNERS, 1994–2003

Opposite
The Great Court has been conceived as a major public space, utilizing areas of the museum previously inaccessible to the general public

Below
Long section, showing how the Great Court forms part of a continuous route through the building

The most prestigious of the many London projects on which Norman Foster was engaged at the turn of the century, the Great Court starts with the basically simple idea of turning an underused open courtyard into a glazed covered space, a central social and circulation focus for the museum; Rick Mather's revamps of the Wallace Collection and, with Building Design Partnership (BDP) engineers, National Maritime Museum are variations on this theme. Modern structural engineering and glazing technology facilitates the operation, providing an economy of means that the Victorians (who invented the idea of the winter garden) lacked.

Where the Great Court scores above both these projects, however, is the fact that it is located in central London, at the heart of one of the most famous – and most visited, and frequently overcrowded – cultural institutions in the world. It was conceived not just as an addition to the amenities of the British Museum but equally as a new public space for London, open late into the evening, a space where you can linger but that also forms the most convenient through route from the London University precinct to Great Russell Street. The huge mass of the museum has become permeable, part of the fabric of the city. For some, the monumental gravitas and the cool – even icy – aesthetic of the space are

a deterrent to relaxing in the café areas – which admittedly seem incidental and somewhat transient, crushed by the grandeur of their surroundings – but the numbers of visitors thronging the Great Court on a typical day make the scheme seem inevitable, the only way in which the museum could sensibly develop for the future.

The British Museum was built in 1823–47 to Greek Revival designs by Sir Robert Smirke. The enfilade of galleries was arranged around the central court, "a dull, miserable looking space" as a contemporary critic described it. In 1854–55 Smirke's brother Sydney constructed the famous Round Reading Room in the middle of the court. Over the next century, all the space around the drum of the Reading Room was filled with bookstacks: the central court became a distant memory. The decision to remove the British Library to a new building at St Pancras – it opened in 1998 – freed up the space around the Reading Room (which itself had to be retained) for museum use. Foster was the winner of a competition held in 1994. Work started on site in spring 1998, and was completed in two and a half years – a considerable achievement in itself.

As part of the project, the much-damaged façades of the court were extensively repaired, and the demolished south portico rebuilt in replica. Foster, in

collaboration with engineers Buro Happold, designed the lightweight roof structure with 3312 glass panels, each one a different size owing to the slightly off-centre placement of the Reading Room in the court. Its structure rests on the perimeter walls and on slender columns buried beneath the new cladding of the drum. The roof provides a calm, even light, regardless of external conditions, and its airy elegance contrasts with the solidity of the great staircases wrapped around the Reading Room, now a public reference library, its original décor carefully reinstated. Education facilities and lecture rooms are buried beneath the floor of the Great Court. A separate, but related, Foster project, due for completion in 2003, will locate new ethnography galleries north of the space, finally breaking down the barrier to circulation imposed by Sir John Burnet's Edward VII Galleries of 1914.

Allowing visitors to 'read' the museum and its extraordinary collections in a new way – traditionally it was a wearying procession of didactic spaces – the Great Court begs comparison with I.M. Pei's ambitious reworking of the Louvre as an exercise in the modernization not only of museum spaces but also of the relationship between the museum and the urban community.

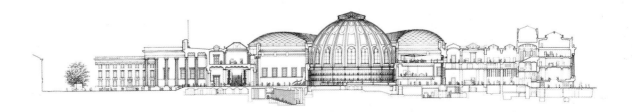

TATE BRITAIN, MILLBANK, SW1
JOHN MILLER & PARTNERS, 1990–2001

John Miller & Partners is one of Britain's most accomplished museum and gallery design practices: it completed a refurbishment of the Serpentine Gallery in 1997 and is currently working on major schemes at the National Gallery of Scotland, Edinburgh, and the Fitzwilliam Museum, Cambridge. The practice's involvement with the Tate began a decade ago with a masterplan for the future development of what was the Tate Gallery, Millbank, and is now, thanks to its director, Nicholas Serota, Tate Britain.

Twentieth-century additions to the original Tate (a dull affair in composite Classical manner, opened in 1897) include, most strikingly, James Stirling's Clore Gallery (1987). Earlier accretions include John Russell Pope's handsome Duveen Gallery and the range of galleries added in the north-eastern corner of the complex by R. Llewellyn-Davies and the Public Services Agency (PSA) in the 1970s. In the early 1980s Jeremy Dixon designed a new basement café (subsequently dismantled). John Miller was responsible for the more recent bookshop and the overhaul of various gallery spaces.

Miller's major Lottery-funded refit of Tate Britain, opened in autumn 2001, provides nine new galleries, three on the main level and six more at basement level, plus a new bookshop, IT room and entrance foyer on Atterbury Street – a natural point of entry for the large numbers of visitors who arrive at the Tate from Pimlico Tube station and

completely accessible to the disabled. (The external landscaping associated with the scheme, including an entrance ramp, has been designed by Allies & Morrison.) Perhaps most significantly, a new triple-height staircase hall now provides a convenient connection between the two levels. The basement (or rather undercroft, since the main level is a *piano nobile*) formerly contained a limited number of galleries (it was easy to overlook them) plus the restaurant, café, cloakrooms and various storage and administrative spaces. An open court behind the Duveen Gallery provided another obvious space for expansion. The galleries embody sophisticated natural and artificial lighting systems, with a system of louvres and solar baffles to control solar gain.

The Tate Britain project represents a vigorous response to the perceived problem – not one that occurs to those who like to see art in comfort – of falling visitor numbers at Millbank (the 'Tate Modern effect'). It will make Tate Britain a more convenient and enjoyable place to visit and address the specific needs of important groups of visitors. Yet the best way of bringing back the visitors may be better exhibitions and a reconsidered hanging policy. Tate Britain will never have the spectacular effect of its sister institution at Bankside, but it contains just as many masterpieces and now possesses the spaces to show them to best effect.

Opposite and top
The new staircase is the most important feature of the project, providing a convenient link between the two main levels of the gallery

Above
Nine new galleries have been provided as part of the new scheme

TATE MODERN, BANKSIDE, SE1

HERZOG & DE MEURON, 1994–2000

The Tate Gallery of Modern Art – subsequently Tate Modern – has been the outstanding success among all the projects generated nationwide by the National Lottery. As other attractions tightened their belts or even closed their doors, Tate Modern boomed – two million people visited during the first three months of opening and the hordes continue to pour in. The (already glittering) career of Sir Nicholas Serota received another boost, as did the ongoing process of regeneration in Southwark. It has helped that admission (except for special exhibitions) is free, and that the new Tate is in London, just across the Thames from St Paul's, and close to a newly opened station on the Jubilee line extension. But the building, like Paris's Pompidou Centre in the 1980s, has become a massive attraction in its own right – ironically enough, since it had been universally condemned when first built. There were those, moreover, who saw the decision to locate the Tate Modern in a converted building, rather than a new landmark design, as a cop-out.

The idea of Tate Modern (controversial in itself) was Nicholas Serota's, and a number of potential sites for a new building were considered. The decision to develop the redundant Bankside power station as a container for the new museum was a matter of common sense. Bankside had been closed for thirteen years (though a massive sub-station along the southern edge of the building remains in use). It was not listed, but Sir Giles Scott's monumental temple of power (completed as recently as 1963) had its admirers. More to the point, it offered all the space the Tate needed, with ample scope for later expansion, and conversion was cheaper than building something new.

An architectural competition was launched in 1994, with the entries whittled down to a shortlist first of thirteen, then of six – Rafael Moneo, Tadao Ando, Renzo Piano, Rem Koolhaas, David Chipperfield and Herzog & de Meuron. Winning Tate Modern catapulted the relatively little-known (at least in Britain) Swiss practice into the front ranks – in 2001, it won the coveted Pritzker Prize.

For the admirers of Scott's building, the winning proposal had its attractions: the external envelope of the power station was to remain largely intact (some competitors had proposed to demolish the prominent chimney and to make radical additions to the exterior). Inside, the vast turbine hall was to be retained as a public forum, entered *via* a huge ramp from the west, with the galleries and other new spaces inserted into the flanking boiler house.

Tate Modern opened in May 2000 amid massive – generally positive – publicity, with the turbine hall filled with an exhibition of large-scale works by the veteran sculptor Louise Bourgeois. A year into its life, the strengths and weaknesses of Herzog & de Meuron's scheme have steadily emerged. The turbine hall itself is a genuinely popular, if rather overwhelming, space. In contrast, the galleries seem too small for the numbers of visitors they attract and lacking in flexibility, while the lifts and escalators are hard pressed to cope with the crowds. The so-called 'grand staircase' – introduced as an afterthought and rather coarsely

detailed – is neither grand nor very helpful as a means of access to the upper floors. The top-floor restaurant is equally inadequate in scale. Herzog & de Meuron's 'light beam', of which the restaurant forms a part, is effectively a corridor, with only partial views across the river to the City. (The best views are obtained from the Tate Friends' room, a level below.) The awkward illuminated cap added to Scott's massive chimney at a late stage in the project is not an adornment: the plan to create a viewing gallery at the top of the stack has not so far been realized.

Yet the defects of the project are outweighed by its sheer bravado and its sophisticated and confident approach to the recycling of an industrial monument, which could easily have vanished (and would have been missed). Moreover, with large areas of the building available for conversion in the future, Tate Modern is an ongoing project of heroic ambition. It has changed the cultural face of London.

Above
The crimson interior of the auditorium contrasts with the subdued hues of the rest of the museum

Opposite
Overlooking the River Thames in Southwark, the building's original turbine hall has been retained, though transformed into a vast public space, while the galleries and ancillary facilities are grouped over seven levels on the north side, accessed by prominent escalators and a discreet staircase

VICTORIA AND ALBERT MUSEUM SPIRAL EXHIBITION ROAD, SW7

DANIEL LIBESKIND/OVE ARUP & PARTNERS, 1998–

Libeskind's Spiral ought to be the most controversial project in London yet, oddly enough, English Heritage, supreme defender of the historic identity of the capital, supports it (as did the former Royal Fine Art Commission), and Kensington and Chelsea Council, never renowned for its innovative taste, gave it planning permission. Even the Victorian Society has been supportive in principle. With its opponents (including a hard core of local residents) apparently vanquished, the only obstacles that the project still has to overcome are financial: there is still a serious shortfall in funding, making the projected completion date of 2004 increasingly doubtful. (The Millennium Commission's dismissal of the Spiral as "insufficiently distinctive" remains incomprehensible – it is distinctive if nothing else.) There is also the wider issue of whether the Spiral should be the highest priority of an institution that has been depicted, rightly or wrongly, as lacking direction and in steady decline.

The Victoria and Albert Museum inhabits a magnificent, but somewhat random, collection of buildings on a site first developed in the aftermath of the 1851 Great Exhibition. Sir Aston Webb's magnificently showy frontage on Cromwell Road, completed in 1909, gives the impression of coherence, but beyond his procession of big spaces, the museum remains an accretion of disparate buildings, the practical problems of which recent masterplanning campaigns (by Michael Hopkins and latterly DEGW) cannot entirely resolve. The site for the Spiral is the Exhibition Road entrance to the museum, which formerly housed the main boilerhouse for the site. More recently, it has been occupied by a single-storey entrance block, linking the main building with the Henry Cole Wing (formerly the Science Schools and dismally converted for museum use by the Property Services Agency in the 1970s). A competition for the development of the site, producing schemes by Zaha Hadid, Nick Grimshaw and others, was won by Libeskind, working with the brilliant Arup director Cecil Balmond, on the back of his acclaimed Berlin Jewish Museum project and in the context, not insignificantly, of Frank Gehry's hugely popular Bilbao Guggenheim.

Superficially irrational and defiant of its surroundings – Exhibition Road is very mixed in quality and in style – the Spiral has a clear, if controversial, agenda: a 'gateway' to the museum, introducing visitors to a global treasure house, a place where contemporary design can be shown alongside the best of the past, a tool allowing the museum to reach new audiences, and a centre for information and interaction, where the latest technology is available to allow anyone to access the breadth of the collections. The conventional gallery spaces in the building are relatively modest in scale. The aspirations of the scheme mirrored the preoccupations of the New Labour government elected in 1997 – education, access and popular appeal above 'élitist' scholarly and curatorial concerns. Having survived the departure of the museum's last director, Alan Borg (its greatest champion), the Spiral has to prove itself in an increasingly pragmatic climate where large Lottery grants are no longer being channelled into cultural projects and at a time when the museum has to make a new régime of free entry attract more visitors to satisfy the Department for Culture, Media and Sport. After three years, the project is beginning to grow stale on the shelf. A decision to build it, or to abandon it and rethink the priorities of the museum, must soon be made.

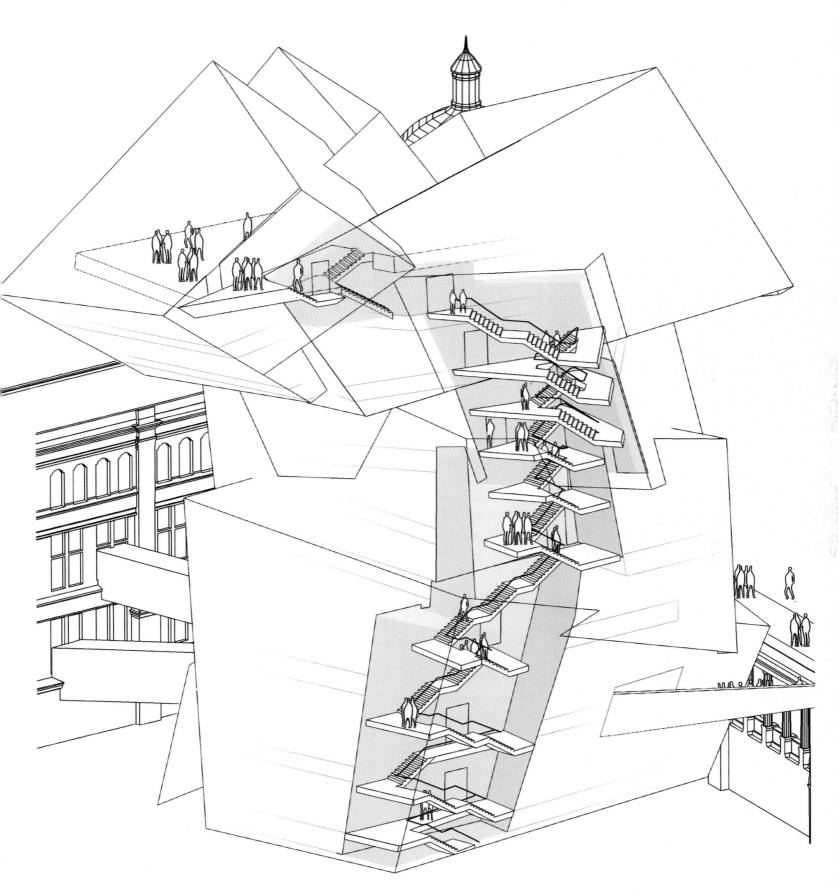

THE WALLACE COLLECTION
MANCHESTER SQUARE, W1

RICK MATHER ARCHITECTS, 1996–2000

The Wallace Collection has an exotic history. It was assembled by four successive marquises of Hertford and left by the Francophile 4th marquis, an eccentric recluse, to his illegitimate son, Sir Richard Wallace, who moved it from Paris to London and installed it in Hertford House. It opened to the public in 1900 and was, at least until recently, one of the least-known major collections in London. The conditions that only the core collection could be shown in the house and that nothing could be loaned for display elsewhere may have blinded Londoners to its enormous quality.

Rick Mather's task – he won the job in a limited competition – was to comprehensively re-equip the Wallace in time for its centenary, addressing issues of security, conservation, access, education and storage; he was also to allow more of the collection to be shown and provide the café and shop that museum visitors now demand, plus a lecture theatre. The site was completely landlocked, making any horizontal extension impossible. The solution was to capitalize on all the underused space within the building, including the rear wing, the basement level and the open court that formed the centre of the mansion. The adaptation of the basement and its connection to the ground floor of the building are skilfully managed – there is now a lecture theatre and a well-equipped education centre.

The typical Victorian museum was understood as a didactic experience, in which the visitor was content to shuffle from room to room, taking in the displays in a prescribed manner. People are no longer so compliant. Like the British Museum Great Court, the glazing-over of the central space at the Wallace Collection allows visitors to break out of the procession of rooms and even to take a coffee or lunch break. On this occasion, the roof does not have the sense of lightness and exhilaration that Mather showed at Dulwich, nor is the space large enough to provide a convincing new dimension to the building. But it has proved attractive enough to pull in local office workers, who have discovered the Wallace as a calm retreat from the tumult of the West End.

Opposite
The redevelopment has not only enclosed a former garden, making it the architectural focus of the museum, but has also opened up former basement levels as galleries and ancillary spaces

Left
The central court, surmounted by a glazed roof, incorporates a restaurant and access to perimeter galleries

WELLCOME WING, THE SCIENCE MUSEUM EXHIBITION ROAD, SW7

MacCORMAC JAMIESON PRICHARD, 1996–2000

Big, bold and blue, Richard MacCormac's Wellcome Wing is a highly efficient, stylish container for a wide range of exhibits and activities that exploits to the full the available space on the Science Museum's cramped site in South Kensington. Not many years ago, MacCormac was best known for his college buildings in Oxford and Cambridge, projects that drew on his strong sense of history, with results that were always interesting but occasionally over-elaborate in their referentiality. Generous budgets, perhaps, might explain this tendency.

The 11,000-square-metre Wellcome Wing, built to a design-and-build contract for just over £21,000,000, is something very different and, together with the superb Southwark Jubilee line station, reflects MacCormac Jamieson Prichard's strong emergence as London architects – the practice's appointment in 2001 as

architects for the redevelopment of the BBC's Broadcasting House site was a further triumph.

The dominant idea behind the Wellcome Wing is flexibility and adaptability – the shape of the building reflects the dynamic nature of the museum's subject-matter. The wing forms an extension westwards of the existing buildings and a further addition, a new conference centre, is planned to terminate the development to the west. An IMAX cinema was one of the facilities to be housed and is conceived as a volume hanging within the space – its sloping auditorium floor is read as a dramatic roof, sweeping up to reveal open galleries on three levels. Construction is tough and simple: concrete columns with steel trusses and steel grilles used extensively as cladding. A huge double-glazed blue-glass window at the west end of the wing fills the interior with a rich but suffused light.

Right
The rich colouring of the Wellcome Wing's interior masks a straightforward rational plan

Opposite
The ceiling, seen here, is formed by the underside of a new auditorium that helps to create a visually exciting space

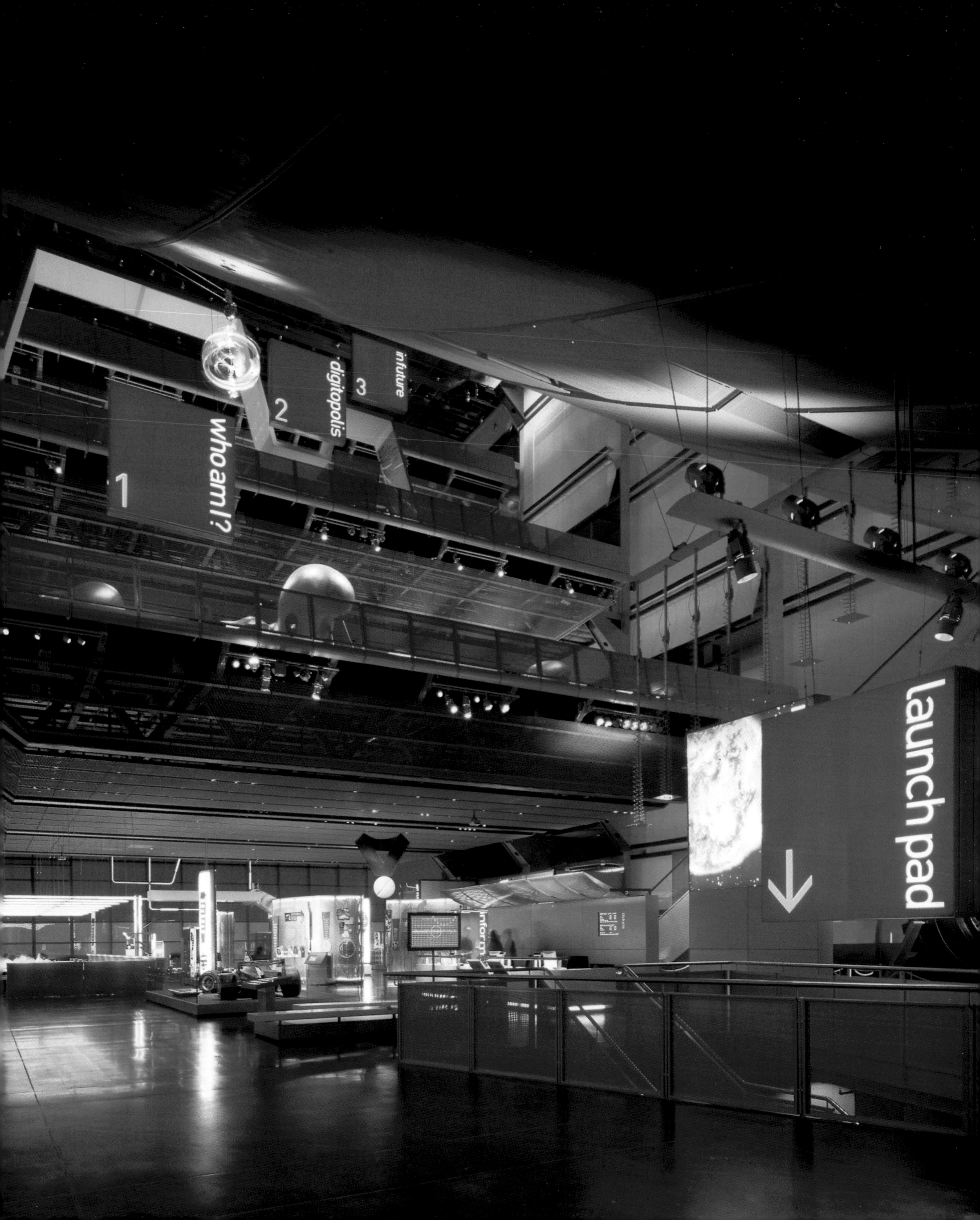
1
who am I?
2
digitopolis
3
in future
launch pad

BATTERSEA POWER STATION
SIR PHILIP DOWSON/ARUP ASSOCIATES/NICHOLAS GRIMSHAW & PARTNERS/
BENOY/BENSON & FORSYTH

BRITISH AIRWAYS LONDON EYE
MARKS BARFIELD ARCHITECTS

CLISSOLD LEISURE CENTRE
HODDER ASSOCIATES

FULHAM FOOTBALL CLUB
SNELL ASSOCIATES

GREAT EASTERN HOTEL
THE MANSER PRACTICE

LABAN DANCE CENTRE
HERZOG & DE MEURON

LONDON CITY RACECOURSE
FOSTER & PARTNERS

LONDON REGATTA CENTRE
IAN RITCHIE ARCHITECTS

MEDIA CENTRE, LORD'S CRICKET GROUND
FUTURE SYSTEMS

PECKHAM LIBRARY
ALSOP ARCHITECTS

THE PLACE
ALLIES & MORRISON

THE ROUNDHOUSE
JOHN McASLAN & PARTNERS

ROYAL COURT THEATRE
HAWORTH TOMPKINS ARCHITECTS

ROYAL FESTIVAL HALL REFURBISHMENT
ALLIES & MORRISON

ROYAL OPERA HOUSE
JEREMY DIXON:EDWARD JONES/BUILDING DESIGN PARTNERSHIP

SADLERS WELLS
ARTS TEAM @ RHWL/NICHOLAS HARE ARCHITECTS

SOHO THEATRE
PAXTON LOCHER ARCHITECTS

TEMPORARY ALMEIDA
HAWORTH TOMPKINS ARCHITECTS

VISITOR CENTRE, QUEEN VICTORIA STREET
JOHN McASLAN & PARTNERS

WEMBLEY STADIUM DEVELOPMENT
FOSTER & PARTNERS/HOK SPORT

BATTERSEA POWER STATION, SW8

SIR PHILIP DOWSON/ARUP ASSOCIATES/NICHOLAS GRIMSHAW & PARTNERS/BENOY/BENSON & FORSYTH, 2001–

Battersea Power Station is a building that is both loved and loathed. For those of a functionalist bent, Giles Scott's architectural coating, which "would have made Telford or Rennie throw up", as Ian Nairn commented, is insufferable. Even admirers of Scott's work regard Bankside (now Tate Modern) as finer. Yet there was general relief, nearly twenty years ago, when listing saved the power station from possible demolition. It is hard to imagine this stretch of the Thames without it.

The subsequent failure of an ambitious project to convert the building into a giant (and very controversial) leisure complex left it bereft, with a side elevation demolished and the interior open to the weather. Since the power station was acquired by Parkview International, a succession of architectural practices has worked on proposals for conversion and for the development of the adjacent, very large (fourteen-hectare) site – the key issue is creating a commercially viable scheme that respects the monumental presence of the listed building. The balance is fine.

The advent of Sir Philip Dowson, formerly of Arup Associates, as masterplanning supremo seems to have welded Parkview's proposals into a balanced scheme that satisfies most interests. The most sensitive element, the conversion of the power station itself, has sensibly been allocated to Nicholas Grimshaw & Partners, working with Benoy. Grimshaw's scheme will turn the building into a huge auditorium suitable for a wide range of events, with subsidiary retail and leisure amenities. Grimshaw does not seek to reinstate the fabric lost in the 1980s, but uses the opportunity created to bring natural light and a sense of space into the interior. All significant surviving features, including a remarkable control room, will be retained.

Grimshaw's emphatic vocabulary of metal and glass is appropriately applied to the design of the new riverside jetty, which incorporates existing industrial remnants, including two fine cranes that are a vital element in the riverside scene. The jetty, constructed on an existing concrete base, is designed to serve a new riverboat service – reflecting a welcome emphasis on public transport – as well as serving as a twenty-first-century version of the Victorian pleasure pier. An ingenious 'see-saw' arrangement is proposed to allow boats to load and unload passengers from 150-seat glazed pods simultaneously.

Above
The new riverside jetty will provide access to a new riverboat service carrying visitors to and from the site

Right
The reconstruction of lost elements of the building will be executed in a lightweight glazed manner, in contrast to Giles Scott's monumental brickwork

BRITISH AIRWAYS LONDON EYE
SOUTH BANK, SE1

MARKS BARFIELD ARCHITECTS, 1993–2000

The idea of the London Eye, perhaps the most popular of all London's millennium projects, emerged late in 1993 when David Marks and Julia Barfield produced proposals for a giant wheel in response to an ideas competition launched by a Sunday newspaper. During 1994 the idea turned into a feasible project as the architects worked on the scheme with engineer Jane Wernick of Arup Associates, forming their own company to build it. A site was found close to County Hall, across the Thames from the Palace of Westminster. The Millennium Wheel, as it was initially described, was controversial – the chairman of the Royal Fine Art Commission, for example, became a vociferous opponent. Nonetheless, Marks Barfield pressed on, enrolling British Airways as a development partner in 1995. Planning consent was given in October 1996, and the search for

specialist collaborators began. Work began on site in January 1999. The plan was to open on New Year's Eve, just under a year later. By summer, the 335-tonne structure was complete, cantilevered off the South Bank and awaiting the final lift. Subsequent delays in lifting the wheel led to its formal opening being postponed until March 2000.

Spanning 135 metres, the height of the spire of Salisbury Cathedral, and carrying thirty-two capsules (each holding up to twenty-five passengers), the Eye is a large object. Yet its impact on the London skyline – it can be seen from Kensington Gardens – is quite ethereal. Moving at a steady half a mile per hour, it provides staggering views across London from the Thames Estuary to Windsor. Some early criticisms of the project focused on the fact that big wheels were nothing new, as George Ferris had set his 120-metre-high wheel spinning in 1893.

The issue turned out to be irrelevant. It was not so much the originality of the idea or the quality of the technology that mattered – and the London Eye is as far removed from a Ferris wheel as a TGV from Puffing Billy – as the piquancy of the siting. Within six months of its opening the Eye had attracted six million visitors. The idea of having pure fun on the South Bank, forgotten since the closure of the Festival of Britain, and peering down on the homes of the Prime Minister and Queen proved irresistible. The Eye is not quite, as some have claimed, the Eiffel Tower of the twenty-first century. It may not be around in a hundred years (though it is unlikely to be dismantled when its limited planning consent expires), but for the moment it is a London sight that everyone wants to see and experience.

Below and opposite
Despite its monumental scale, the British Airways London Eye has a delicate presence on the London skyline

CLISSOLD LEISURE CENTRE
CLISSOLD ROAD, STOKE NEWINGTON, N16

HODDER ASSOCIATES, 1996–2001

The swimming pool at Colne, Lancashire, was the building that first brought Manchester-based Stephen Hodder to national attention – he later won the first-ever Stirling Prize for his Centenary Building at Salford University. The Clissold Leisure Centre reflects the increasing redefinition of sports facilities as civic and community centres and urban markers.

Hodder won the commission in 1996. The building opened in autumn 2001. The site is close to Clissold Park, in what was a solid Victorian suburb, sadly damaged by random demolition. The area is typical of much of inner London and of the borough of Hackney in particular: far from affluent and home to a number of ethnic groups, some with very specific needs. The special circumstances of the area guaranteed generous funding for the project, including a substantial Lottery grant.

Hodder's aim was to design "a real urban building, part of a process of reconstructing the street – a shed was the last thing that was needed". The building should be a landmark, though a highly practical one, designed for easy maintenance and low running costs. The diagram is idiosyncratic while reflecting a functional brief. A weighty, cruciform, concrete-framed core – the architect concedes there is an element here of homage to Corbusier – sits within a clear-span, steel-framed, highly glazed envelope. The core holds the support and service functions, and the surrounding lightweight envelope contains the performance spaces: a competition standard swimming pool, training pool and sports hall. Making optimum use of natural light was an important objective in the scheme, while by night the building is intended to shine as a lantern, proclaiming the value of physical exercise. The aluminium-clad roof shines externally and internally, with its 30-metre span supported on Y-columns. Look out for a very specific Corb reference: a tiled bench in the pool area modelled on that in the bathroom of the Villa Savoye. Having provided Hackney with a high-value, stylish community resource, Hodder should be forgiven for a visual joke that few users of the centre are likely to comprehend.

Opposite and left
The building contrasts the monumental and the lightweight, with the optimum use of daylight in the performance and training spaces a prime objective of the design

FULHAM FOOTBALL CLUB, SW6

SNELL ASSOCIATES, 1998–2004

Below and opposite, top left
The futuristic form of the stadium sits close to
the River Thames, among streets of small-scale
suburban houses

Opposite, top right and bottom
The development extends the public domain
along the Thames, with glimpses from the riverside
walkway into the ground

The Fulham Football Club ground, popularly
known as Craven Cottage after a villa that
survives on the site, has been the subject of
numerous development proposals over the
last twenty years. Quinlan Terry's proposal
to create a version of Richmond Riverside
there was rejected after a public inquiry.

In contrast, Robin Snell's scheme
provides for a development that will retain
the present use of the site, while giving the
club and its supporters vastly improved
facilities in line with their ambitions.

The context of the scheme is the Grade
II listing of Craven Cottage and of the late
Victorian stand and the proximity of a
public park (itself listed) and of the River
Thames. The ground sits in an area of
dense housing development, and scale
is an issue: the rebuilt ground will
accommodate no more than 30,000
spectators, half the capacity of some of
Britain's larger football venues.

The existing stand has a handsome
street frontage but is essentially a utilitarian
structure that does not meet present-day
standards of amenity and safety. It is to be
demolished, except for the street front, with
a new stand, of striking form, constructed
like a bowl within the frame of the Victorian
brickwork. The structural system allows for
a high degree of transparency, with
glimpses right through to the pitch from the
riverside walkway. Robin Snell, whose time
in the office of Michael Hopkins culminated
in the role of project architect for
Glyndebourne, describes the ethos of
the ground as "more Lord's than Stamford
Bridge". He has created an almost
theatrical setting for a sport that is
increasingly generating outstanding
architecture.

GREAT EASTERN HOTEL
LIVERPOOL STREET, EC2

THE MANSER PRACTICE, 1995–2000

The Great Eastern Hotel was described by Sir John Betjeman, lover of all things Victorian, as "the only hotel in the City, and a very good one". The hotel was built, adjacent to Liverpool Street station, in the 1880s and extended by R.W. Edis in 1901. The lack of adequate connections between the two parts of the hotel was always a problem, though the Great Eastern retained its solid reputation into the post-war years. More recently, starved of investment, it declined into a backwater. The Manser Practice's client for the £65,000,000 refurbishment completed in 2000 was a consortium that included design and restaurant magnate Sir Terence Conran. Five new restaurants and bars were included in the reconstruction, which also increased the number of guest rooms by 40%.

The radical upgrading of the listed building included not only the renewal of all services and complete external restoration, but also the total rebuilding of the top two floors, where a new roof structure is punctuated by circular 'bull's eye' *oculi*, designed in the spirit of the Victorians. The reception was relocated eastwards, with a circular lightwell cut into its ceiling and extending to the top of the hotel. The key move in the scheme was, however, the creation of a striking atrium at first-floor level, linking the previously disconnected wings and giving the Great Eastern a new social hub. Many of the bedrooms look down into this space, which contains a carefully detailed lift shaft, clad in perforated metal mesh, to which the main boiler flue, made of polished stainless steel, is attached.

The revived Great Eastern appeals to City tastes – high style combined with a reassuring emphasis on comfort. This is no designer hotel, yet the marriage of an historic institution with modern design sets a lead for the renewal of other big nineteenth-century London hotels.

Opposite and left
The newly constructed atrium, with its striking lift and boiler shafts, now forms the core of the hotel, and is overlooked by a number of the bedrooms

LABAN DANCE CENTRE, CREEKSIDE, SE8

HERZOG & DE MEURON, 1997–2002

The Zürich-based partnership of Herzog & de Meuron – winners of the 2001 Pritzker Prize for Architecture – scored a notable victory with its appointment for the conversion of Bankside power station into Tate Modern. It is appropriate that this landmark scheme – a great popular success – is now being followed up by a more modest, but perhaps even more innovative, project based in south-east London, a few miles down-river from Bankside.

Herzog & de Meuron won the commission for the Laban Centre in competition in 1997, presumably on the back of its triumph at the Tate. The brief provided for a three-hundred-seat dance theatre, twelve studios (some suitable for public performances), lecture rooms, library and archives, community spaces and café/bar. The site is on Deptford Creek, once a centre of shipbuilding but in recent decades the picture of urban dereliction. That, hopefully, is set to change. Better communications and the impact of regeneration in nearby Greenwich has made developers look seriously at Deptford. The Creekside site is far from remote and Thomas Archer's noble Baroque church of St Paul, Deptford, is a short walk away. The Laban Centre, promoting the principles of the thinker and teacher Rudolf Laban, had moved to New Cross from Surrey in 1975 and was firmly rooted in south-east London, keen to be part of the regeneration of the area.

The architects envisage the Centre as "a small city, with streets, mews, squares, courtyards – a congestion of spaces. Somewhere that addresses all the senses". Beginning with a detailed study of the existing Laban premises, they evolved the idea of a 'village' of studios, spaces that are naturally lit by day but that appear, after dark, as beacons to the surrounding area. The Centre, they say, should be "a lantern at night, a place of movement and change". The project has been developed in collaboration with artist Michael Craig-Martin (formerly an influential teacher at nearby Goldsmiths College, the point of departure for the new British art scene). The use of colour is an integral ingredient. Layered glazing, which makes use of innovative manufacturing technology, provides a cinematographic effect, where dancers can be seen as shadows through the curving glass façade.

The Laban project, which looked pioneering when launched, has already generated new investment and commercial development in the immediate vicinity; as far as locals are concerned, the infusion of Lottery and other public funding has been well justified. A programme of community activities is promised when the new building opens in 2002. But the greatest gain for London as a whole will be a major work by a practice that is using technology to rekindle the art of architecture.

Above
The curving glass façade, colourful by day and transparent by night, opens up the centre to this historic yet underprivileged district of south-east London

LONDON CITY RACECOURSE, BARKINGSIDE

FOSTER & PARTNERS, 2001–03

Below
The grandstand, capable of accommodating up to 10,000 spectators, rises to a high point close to the finishing line, the logical centre of attention at any racecourse

It is three-quarters of a century since an entirely new racecourse was opened in Britain. Some of the major venues – Goodwood, Epsom, and Ascot – are engaged in major building campaigns to update their facilities, but the typical British racecourse is an accretion of elements that have been brought together over a long period, with no special regard to the convenience of most spectators. (Indeed, until recently, the needs of the typical race-goer seemed to be an afterthought at best.)

Foster's proposed London City Racecourse represents a typical Foster strategy of rethinking the function and format of a venue from scratch. The centrepiece is the grandstand, a structure with all the dynamism of form that Foster would apply to an airport. It can accommodate ten thousand spectators, with a further ten thousand mostly using covered facilities. The form of the roof is conceived to intensify the excitement of the race while containing the activities of the course and shielding nearby residential areas from noise. The stable block is not, as is usual, tucked away out of sight, but located directly in front of the grandstand, across the course, so that all can see the horses being led into the parade ring. Lifts within the stand can whisk spectators to roof level, where there is a vast panorama of the course, east London and the City beyond. The form of the stand is echoed in other buildings across the site, including a health club, crèche and restaurant block, while the provision of facilities for sailing and golf broaden the appeal (and funding base) of the development.

LONDON REGATTA CENTRE
DOCKSIDE ROAD, E14

IAN RITCHIE ARCHITECTS, 1997–99

The powerful Jubilee line station at Bermondsey aside, Ian Ritchie's built works in London are surprisingly modest in scale – a concert platform at Crystal Palace, for example, and interiors at the Natural History Museum – which is one reason to include his project of the late 1990s here. The Regatta Centre was one of the first new buildings of significant quality to be completed in the long-closed Royal Docks. The site is on Royal Albert Dock, where there is a 2000-metre Olympic-standard rowing course – one good use for a redundant dock.

The Royals are far removed from Henley-on-Thames, and Ritchie's centre is a tough beast made of robust materials and unawed by its setting, yet the detailing is characteristically careful and even delicate. There are, in fact, two buildings here: a clubhouse, with changing rooms, short-stay accommodation and a practice rowing tank, and a boathouse, where up to eighty boats can be stored, plus workshop for repairs and maintenance. The linear form of the complex reflects the nature of the site, squeezed against the water by the elevated track of the Docklands Light Railway. The sharp nose of the clubhouse, highly glazed and open to the dockside, the rear elevation a stark composition in fair-faced concrete, responds to the line of the water. The boathouse is a plain rectangle. Its construction is remarkably straightforward: steel columns, with brackets to support the stored boats, hold up a stainless-steel sheet roof. The walls of the building are gabions – metal cages filled with rough stones. The gabion wall on the north side of the clubhouse encloses a long access spine. This "ambulatory", as Ritchie describes it, is a memorable space: enclosed between rough stonework and smooth concrete, floored in timber and lit from above.

MEDIA CENTRE
LORD'S CRICKET GROUND, NW1

FUTURE SYSTEMS, 1995–99

Older than most of the completed projects included in this book, yet still an astonishingly futuristic sight, the Lord's Media Centre could hardly be described as anything but 'contemporary'. It is the latest of a series of progressive commissions by the Marylebone Cricket Club (MCC), beginning with Michael Hopkins's Mound Stand in the 1980s and including, more recently, Nicholas Grimshaw's effortlessly elegant

Grand Stand, opened in 1998, as well as a number of smaller structures by David Morley Architects (also responsible for the development masterplan for the ground).

The new media centre was planned to open in time for the 1999 Cricket World Cup held at Lord's, providing space for up to one hundred and twenty broadcasters and journalists. An invited competition for its design was held in 1995 and won by

Future Systems, a practice that moved in the 1990s from inspirational ideas to completed buildings. While Hopkins and Grimshaw were recognizably working in an updated version of the engineering tradition of the Victorian period, Future Systems envisaged their building as a lightweight object, prefabricated off-site, like a yacht or aircraft, using a semi-monocoque technique – an aluminium skin forms the

structure of the building, being stiffened with aluminium ribs. The centre sits on two concrete legs, containing stairs and lifts and clad in GRP, between the Compton and Edrich stands (relatively matter-of-fact additions by Hopkins). The external skin is spray-painted a brilliant white. Inside, the commentators' seats are ranged in tiers, like those of the spectators below. The ice-blue colour scheme, apparently somewhat compromised since the opening of the building, was chosen to instil an air of calm (though air conditioning ensures cool conditions). The angled all-glass front of the centre was designed to prevent glare, a potential distraction to players.

This remains Future Systems' largest built project in London. Its smooth, slightly sinister quality makes it unmissable and unforgettable, a "loveable alien", as the *Architects' Journal* described it.

Left
The ranks of seating ensure that the world's press have the clearest possible view of the cricket pitch below

Opposite
The smooth and striking form of the building's exterior builds on the techniques developed in the construction of aeroplanes and boats

PECKHAM LIBRARY, PECKHAM SQUARE, SE15
ALSOP ARCHITECTS, 1998–2000

Asked why the Peckham Library and Media Centre is raised twelve metres above Peckham Square, a new public space intended as a focus for community life and regeneration in this underprivileged area of south London, Will Alsop is apt to reply: "why not?" In fact, the logic behind the move becomes apparent to anyone who ascends to the library. There are views not only of the square and surrounding area but also, through the highly transparent, multi-coloured northern elevation, of the public and commercial monuments of the City and West End a few miles away; Peckham's

perceived isolation from central London is revealed as, in fact, an illusion. The overhang of the library shelters part of the square from the weather. Elevated above the streets, the library is both part of the urban fabric and, at the same time, a place appealingly apart, a semi-secret world that has a particular attraction for young people. Public libraries were traditionally seen as places where the masses could be educated and 'improved' – a worthy ideal, but too paternalistic and condescending for the twenty-first century. The Peckham Library is unashamedly colourful, shapely

and sensuous: a container for a new approach to education and information.

The library itself, clad in green patinated copper with a prominent red 'tongue' at roof level, cantilevers out from a five-storey vertical block containing the entrance lobby, offices and staff facilities and a multi-media centre for IT training. Within the reading room, three timber pods set on stilts house a meeting room, children's activity area and a specialist Afro-Caribbean library. The building has presence and glamour, but is far from extravagant; the naturally ventilated interior is equally made for low-cost running.

This is a building for the local community, wearing its serious purpose lightly and reflecting Alsop's conviction that architecture must be interesting, stimulating, unforgettable as well as functional. Peckham Library is all those things and more. It is a building that has a great deal to say about the city, the relationship between learning and enjoyment and the place of art in architecture.

Opposite
The library's interior provides a new and stimulating environment at the heart of the community in which to read and learn

Right and below
The north elevation provides a colourful and transparent beacon that looks towards the City and the West End, while the south elevation shelters the new square that has been developed as a focus for this deprived inner-city community

THE PLACE, DUKE'S ROAD, WC1

ALLIES & MORRISON, 1995–2001

Allies & Morrison's skilful reconstruction of The Place re-equips a well-liked and successful venue for dance without removing its informal and ad hoc character. The 1880s Drill Hall (built for the Artists' Rifles) has been used by the Contemporary Dance Trust since 1969, since when it has expanded its activities into adjacent buildings. The Place is a centre for performance and training, in use from early morning to late in the evening.

Allies & Morrison's involvement with The Place began in 1995, when the practice began work on a masterplan for future development. This led to a £5,000,000 Lottery grant, which was used as the basis for further fundraising. A new entrance for performers and students has been created on Flaxman Terrace, a dramatic triple-height space beyond which dancers can be glimpsed by passers-by. The dance studios have been comprehensively overhauled and equipped with new services

Right and opposite
The Place, a classic example of the creative use of an old building, has been given a new public face with the addition of a three-storey entrance pavilion, while the existing performance and rehearsal spaces have been refurbished

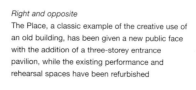

THE ROUNDHOUSE, CHALK FARM ROAD, NW1

JOHN McASLAN & PARTNERS, 1998–2004

The Roundhouse is one of the great industrial monuments of London. It was built in 1847 as an engine shed serving the London and Birmingham Railway; redundant within twenty years, it was converted into a warehouse and remained in this use for nearly a century. In 1964 the building passed into the hands of Arnold Wesker's Centre 42 and entered a new incarnation as a venue for experimental theatre, rock music and 'happenings', all of which were in tune with its bare industrial aesthetic. The building was effectively used 'as found': few changes or improvements were made and only the most basic maintenance was carried out. By the 1980s the Roundhouse

was in liquidation, with Camden Council and the GLC stepping in to acquire it. The GLC proposed to use it to establish a centre for black artists, but efforts to secure a permanent purpose for the building came to nothing. More recently Michael Hopkins prepared a scheme to convert it into a home for the RIBA's drawings collection: this would have involved extensive internal change to accommodate large areas of storage space, reading rooms and offices. The use of the building by conceptual artists and performance groups has emphasized the need to protect its spatial qualities.

Philanthropist Torquil Norman bought the Roundhouse in 1998 with the aim of

making it into an arts centre for young people and held a limited competition to select an architect. John McAslan's Lottery-backed project focuses on the retention and restoration of the building's great internal space, to be used as a flexible performance area, with studios in the undercroft. Support facilities are contained within a new, crescent-shaped building, lightly joined to the Roundhouse: the aim is to preserve the great brick drum uncompromised. After decades of uncertainty, this iconic north London landmark appears to have a bright future.

Opposite
Views of working model, showing interior levels (basement, auditorium and mezzanine) and roof

Right
Interior cutaway view of working model, showing how the insertion of new facilities has been balanced with the desire to retain the internal and external integrity of the historic structure

ROYAL COURT THEATRE
SLOANE SQUARE, SW3

HAWORTH TOMPKINS ARCHITECTS, 1995–2000

Below
West–east section, showing restaurant beneath
Sloane Square, left, and the theatre, right

A slender new building containing offices and
dressing-rooms has been clamped on to the side
of the existing building

Opposite
A characteristic of the refurbishment has been
the retention of many of the interior finishes and
surfaces, as found, giving the building a rich
and varied palette and texture

The Royal Court Theatre has been famous since the 1950s as a venue for innovative, mould-breaking productions. (It was here that John Osborne's *Look Back in Anger* premiered.) The theatre itself, though listed Grade II, is not of outstanding architectural interest: its fussy 1880s façade makes little impression on Sloane Square and certainly does not challenge the sleekly elegant curve of Peter Jones on the end of the King's Road.

Haworth Tompkins' reconstruction of the theatre confronted a number of difficult issues, quite apart from the confined character of the site. The distressed, not to say scruffy, ambience of the interior was widely seen as part of its charm, and nobody wanted it sanitized. But facilities for English Stage Company staff, performers and audiences were very poor. The scheme added a new six-storey block of dressing rooms and offices alongside the main building, with more accommodation in a deep basement. The upstairs studio theatre was totally rebuilt. A considerable slice of the budget went into the construction of a new bar and restaurant under the square (replacing an existing public convenience) with an entrance from the central paved area as well as from the theatre. The local authority's subsequent refusal to allow access from the square was, to say the least, perverse.

The main façade remains largely unchanged, except for cleaning and new lighting. Inside the theatre, the approach was one of stripping back dilapidated and poor-quality finishes, leaving old brickwork and new concrete exposed, so that the interior is a place of rich and memorable texture. A new main staircase is constructed of thin, stepped concrete spans, meticulously detailed. The effect is Scarpa-esque, a contrast to the sleek look of many new/old schemes. Audiences and actors appear to like the rebuilt Court – the spirit of the place lives on.

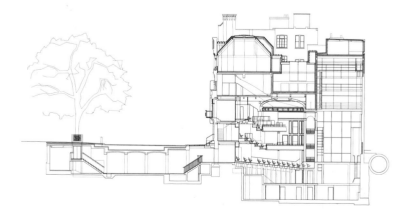

ROYAL FESTIVAL HALL REFURBISHMENT
BELVEDERE ROAD, SE1
ALLIES & MORRISON, 1992–

The appointment of Allies & Morrison to implement a progressive programme of repair and reinstatement at the Royal Festival Hall, the only surviving building from the 1951 Festival of Britain, is one of the key achievements to date of the South Bank Board, which took charge of the entire South Bank Centre after the demise of the Greater London Council (GLC). (At the time of writing, a far bigger project, the implementation of Rick Mather's masterplan for the entire South Bank site, has yet to start, leaving the Royal Festival Hall stranded in an area that is conspicuously in limbo and beginning to show the detrimental effects of many years of indecision.)

"The prime monument of the Welfare State era" , as historian Elain Harwood has described the Grade I listed hall, is a perennially popular, beautifully made, and highly subtle building that marries the optimism and drive of the post-war years, when the Modern Movement moved centre-stage in Britain, with the decorative and craft-oriented preoccupations of an older tradition, transmuted *via* the medium of Scandinavia. The form of the building, with its 'egg in a box' auditorium surrounded by open foyers, was the conception of Leslie Martin, while the interiors were designed by a London County Council (LCC) team led by Peter Moro. Both men were still alive and able to offer advice and encouragement when Allies & Morrison began working on the Royal Festival Hall in the early 1990s. There was general dissatisfaction with the changes implemented by the GLC in 1963–65, which extended the river front of the building, imposing bland new elevations, and wrapped it in a network of walkways and service roads in line with then-current ideas of pedestrian/vehicle segregation. The 'open foyers' policy of the 1980s GLC opened the building to all, from early morning to late evening – today, the majority of the Royal Festival Hall's users never attend a concert there. Peter Moro welcomed this revolution, while deploring the uncontrolled invasion of the public spaces by the shops and cafés that followed the influx of people.

Allies & Morrison (who produced an exceptionally well-considered submission for the 1994 South Bank masterplanning competition) seem to have a natural sympathy with the Royal Festival Hall; their own roots are in the Cambridge school which Leslie Martin made into such a potent architectural force. Their proposals have been developed in conservation plans published in 1996 and 2000. Early phases of work reinstated the character of the original (west) entrance foyer and the progression from entrance to principal level and created an elegant new restaurant overlooking the river. A stretch of 1960s walkway masking the hall from Belvedere Road was removed. There were plans to finally create the grand south entrance that Martin had wanted, but these have since been dropped in favour of a new café opening on to a festival square. It is accepted that the changes of the 1960s cannot be entirely undone, but the reopening of terraces and balconies at the upper levels of the building will recreate something of the openness of the original.

A prime objective is the clearance of catering and retail outlets that clutter the public spaces.

Since 1999 Allies & Morrison have worked closely with South Bank masterplanner Rick Mather, since the Royal Festival Hall cannot be detached from its context. The masterplan provides for the suppression of the 1960s service roads around the hall and the insertion, along the edge of the Hungerford railway viaduct, of a new administrative and retail block, designed by Allies & Morrison, which will provide space to decant offices and shops from the Royal Festival Hall. The most daunting element in the £50,000,000 refurbishment scheme is undoubtedly the overhaul of the auditorium, which has acoustics that are now regarded as defective. This means closing the space for a season or two, and it seems imperative that at least one of the other auditoriums planned for the site is ready for use before closure takes place.

Below
Allies & Morrison's ongoing refurbishment project aims to restore the interior of the Royal Festival Hall in line with the intentions of its original architects and to reverse some of the detrimental changes made since 1951

Right
The opening of the People's Palace restaurant, along the river front of the building, made good use of one of the spaces created as a result of the 1960s extension, but its style was a deliberate throwback to the lighter aesthetic of 1951

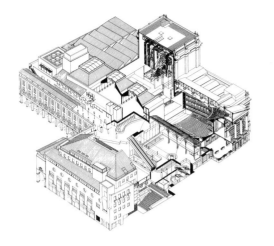

Opposite
The Floral Hall, previously a pathetic remnant, has been partially rebuilt and given a new rôle as part of the development

Right
As this cutaway shows, the project involved not only the substantial rebuilding of the opera house, but also the reconstruction of the entire block

Below
A new internal route, containing the box office, links Covent Garden piazza with Bow Street

ROYAL OPERA HOUSE COVENT GARDEN, WC2

JEREMY DIXON:EDWARD JONES/ BUILDING DESIGN PARTNERSHIP, 1984–2000

The Royal Opera House is reckoned one of the great opera houses of the world, yet it became the home of a national opera company (and dance company) only after the Second World War. The present theatre is the third to occupy the site, close to the Covent Garden piazza, a pioneering exercise in urban design by Inigo Jones and now the heartland of tourist London. Built in 1857–58 to designs by E.M. Barry, the Royal Opera House is a much-loved musical shrine. After more than a century of use, however, its facilities proved increasingly inadequate for modern needs. Following twenty years of discussion, the first phase of an extension programme was completed in 1982 by GMW architects, by which time a more ambitious development scheme was being planned. Jeremy Dixon and William Jack (of Building Design Partnership) won the competition held in 1984, narrowly beating Edward Cullinan and Richard Rogers. After 1989 the project was developed by the partnership of Dixon and Edward Jones, in conjunction with Building Design Partnership (with Charles Broughton as design director). The scheme went through several major transformations before work started on site in 1996 – in its first incarnation, half of the space on the 2.5-acre site was allotted for commercial development, a Thatcherite strategy for funding the development without recourse to public funds that was hotly opposed by community activists. The built scheme, which is devoted, apart from some retail space, to ROH use (the backstage areas are vast), was made possible by a large and controversial Lottery grant, plus substantial private donations.

Jeremy Dixon regards the ROH project as being as much about urban planning as theatre design. It became, he says, "a complex procedure of collaging … a compressed version of the natural development of a city". One element that remained constant in the various reworkings of the scheme was the run of new façades replacing the long-lost frontages of Inigo Jones's piazza. Where other architects proposed replicas of the vanished original, Dixon produced a reinterpretation in a stripped classical manner. In the angle of the piazza, a new entrance leads into the theatre, restoring an arrangement that prevailed in pre-Barry days.

On Russell Street and Bow Street, the architectural style hangs somewhere between rationalism and straightforward modern – the disjunction on Russell Street between this manner and that of the piazza frontages is deliberate. On Bow Street, the Barry portico (with a clumsy 1930s conservatory unfortunately left blocking the colonnade) and the restored frontage of the 1860 Floral Hall – which had been half demolished after a 1956 fire – dominate. The idea of using the Vilar Floral Hall (as it became) as a great public foyer for all the house's patrons – breaking down the divisions between the various parts of the auditorium was a key theme of the scheme – was an inspired notion. Yet the fact that it is raised up to allow for a major service entrance on to Bow Street makes it seem inaccessible, and the route into the hall is far from direct. The supposed 'opening up' of the ROH to the general public has been, in the event, rather half-hearted. The most successful element in the reconstruction is the device of an escalator link, whisking patrons direct to a striking top-level bar – but again the route from the street is, perhaps deliberately, indirect. The auditorium, of course, remains unchanged, apart from a repaint and reseating operation, and the mystique and the exclusiveness of the ROH have not been erased by the rebuilding. For London, however, this exercise in Post-modern urban design has real benefits: the piazza façades have an inevitability that made them an immediate and accepted part of the historic Covent Garden scene.

SADLERS WELLS, ROSEBERY AVENUE, EC1

ARTS TEAM @ RHWL/NICHOLAS HARE ARCHITECTS, 1995–98

The arrival of the National Lottery, launched by John Major's otherwise sterile administration, transformed the arts scene in Britain. Popular science centres (Magna, the Earth Centre, Dynamic Earth and so on) blossomed around the country, and in London a massive grant was awarded, amidst considerable controversy, to rebuild the Royal Opera House. The Lottery seemed to be a bottomless coffer.

Under New Labour, the Lottery has been substantially rethought and funds redirected towards projects that might traditionally have been funded from taxation – no more ROH-style spending sprees. Completed as long ago as 1998, the reconstruction of Sadlers Wells demonstrated the potential for fast-track, good-value arts projects, with operational issues more important than those of high style. In this context, it provides a benchmark for the future; similar thinking informs Arts Team @RHWL's forthcoming refit of the London Coliseum.

The new Sadlers Wells, opened late in 1998, is the fifth theatre on the site – the first opened in 1683. Its 1931 predecessor, though much-loved, was externally forgettable, internally cramped, and, though listed (for its associations), regarded as expendable. Its context was extremely mixed: across Rosebery Avenue is Berthold Lubetkin's heroic Spa Green Estate. The aim behind the reconstruction was to re-equip the theatre operationally and technically, with vastly improved facilities for audiences and performers; to maintain the special character of the 'Wells' as a local institution, but equally to give it a new image and widen the audience base. Nicholas Hare's street frontage, with brick planes framing a glazed entrance elevation, does the job efficiently: after dark, the foyer opens up invitingly to the street. The twenty-six-metre-high flytower is not suppressed but frankly expressed as a marker on Rosebery Avenue. At the rear of the building, on Arlington Way, projecting windows break the façade, providing passers-by with glimpses into the interior. Hare is an adept urban compositionalist, and here he is on good form.

Nicholas Thompson of the Arts Team, responsible for the interior of the building, retained the existing placing of the auditorium, keeping part of the structure for purely practical reasons. But the new auditorium is a highly original, slightly frightening place – none of the reassurance, for instance, of Hopkins's Glyndebourne – steeply raked, devoid of traditional frills, starkly clad in perforated metal, its challenging austerity slightly relieved by colourful seat coverings. (But Sadlers Wells, unlike Glyndebourne, is a mould-breaking place.) The foyer is seen as a single space, with lightweight galleries floating in the volume – in practice, this is perhaps a slightly disorientating area, with too many levels and no clear focus of activity. Yet the overall effect of the development is to refresh and reinvigorate an old friend, and the anticipated broadening of horizons is already well under way.

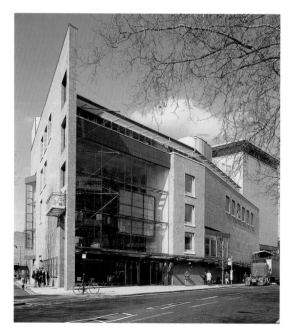

SOHO THEATRE, DEAN STREET, W1

PAXTON LOCHER ARCHITECTS, 1996–2000

Lottery funding underpinned a number of high-profile, high-cost arts projects launched in Britain during the late 1990s; the Royal Opera House provides the most striking example in London. The Soho Theatre's Lottery funding was far more modest and the company's translation to a new home was accomplished *via* a shrewd mix of public funding and straightforward property speculation that allows it to channel such future subsidies as it can raise directly into productions. Its overheads are covered by the revenue from the building.

The company's search for a new base began in 1995, when it was obliged to quit the Cockpit Theatre. It settled on a former synagogue in the heart of Soho, a decent seven-storey block with a sizeable worship space at its core. Paxton Locher, with no previous experience of theatre design, was selected from a shortlist of six practices. The strategy was to place the new, 200-seat auditorium at first- and second-floor level, suspended in space, as it were. The ground floor and basement house the box office, bar and restaurant. The third floor contains rehearsal and administrative space, with apartments on the top three floors (which step back on the rear elevation). The return from the residential development underwrote the project. The result of this approach has been to produce a mixed-use building, a microcosm of the city and a striking contrast to the arts ghettos of the Barbican and South Bank. The ethos of the building suits the company, with its emphasis on new and experimental work and its desire to break out of the traditional theatrical mould.

The changes to the existing building were subtle and respectful: a lightweight canopy to the street, a delicate steel framework denoting the theatre space (with the control room expressed as a box on the street elevation) and a set-back penthouse at roof level. The auditorium is a highly flexible black box, with steeply raked bench seating; the emphasis on intimacy and communication between audience and actors. Paxton Locher, still best known, perhaps, for their exquisite house and studio in Clerkenwell, proved that specialist experience is not always the route to an inspired job.

TEMPORARY ALMEIDA
PENTONVILLE ROAD, N1

HAWORTH TOMPKINS ARCHITECTS, 2001

The reconstruction of the highly successful Almeida Theatre's Islington base – a project estimated to extend over a minimum of eighteen months – posed a problem for the management. One alternative was to lease a West End theatre, but the ethos of the West End is out of tune with the Almeida's style. Instead, a temporary auditorium has been created in King's Cross. The yard behind the seedy Pentonville Road had been used as a bus station and car repair depot. There were no on-site services. The budget was extremely low. The final cost of the temporary theatre was £800,000 for 230 square metres of space, with two auditoriums of distinctively different character created and most of the cost going to services. The lightweight structure has a sophistication that belies its modest cost – the translucent screen enclosing the foyer is an attractive device.

Temporary cultural facilities have a knack of becoming semi-permanent; Frank Gehry's Temporary Contemporary in Los Angeles is a good example. Perhaps the

Temporary Almeida will carry on when the original Almeida reopens. The project has already demonstrated the potential for a process of gradual renewal of the rundown area around King's Cross station, where crudely insensitive plans for total redevelopment have been opposed by heritage and community groups. With the right formula, a mix of uses, refurbishment combined with infilling of gap sites, this area could blossom.

Haworth Tompkins (best known for the reconstruction of the Royal Court, see pp. 108–09) has become a leading theatre-design practice. In 2000 it fitted out a temporary auditorium for the Almeida in the old Gainsborough Studios before work started on a mixed-use conversion of the building. Its refurbishment of the Open Air Theatre in Regent's Park, designed with landscape practice Camlin Lonsdale, has infused new life and a sense of delight into a worthy but tired 1970s facility, making a visit to the park something of an adventure.

Right and opposite
Seen as a temporary facility, using cheap materials with a sense of style, the theatre has been inserted into a disused yard in King's Cross

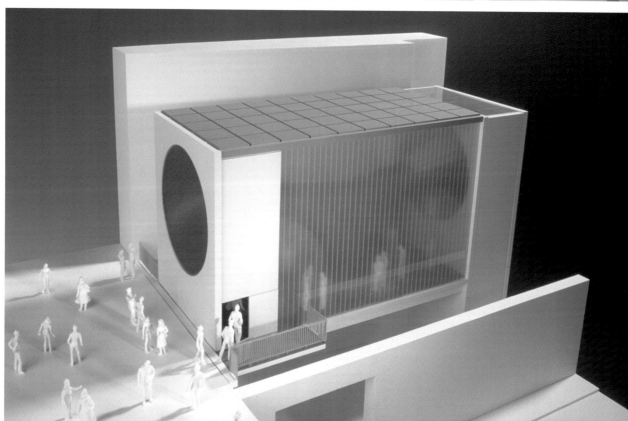

VISITOR CENTRE
QUEEN VICTORIA STREET, EC4
JOHN McASLAN & PARTNERS, 1999–2002

This remarkable collaborative work, involving artist Anish Kapoor, has been generated by the decision of the Salvation Army to quit the City site that it has occupied since the days of General William Booth and sell the land there for redevelopment. A new office scheme will replace the existing 1960s building, which succeeded the original headquarters destroyed by wartime bombing. McAslan's visitor centre capitalizes on a prime location on the pedestrian route from St Paul's to Tate Modern, *via* the Millennium Bridge. It incorporates an exhibition about the global work of the Salvation Army on a lower level, but the most striking feature of the project is the pavilion designed in association with Kapoor as a place for contemplation, effectively a huge piece of sculpture. The fluted form is fabricated of CorTen steel: you can walk through it or linger. There are views of the fine tower (all that survived the Second World War) of Wren's church of St Mary Somerset. The structure brings together the past, present and future of the City in a memorable work by a major modern artist whose work is rooted in tradition.

Opposite and right
Located on the pedestrian route connecting St Paul's Cathedral with Tate Modern *via* the Millennium Bridge, the Salvation Army's Visitor Centre is a place of contemplation as well as information, and represents a fertile collaboration between artist and architect

WEMBLEY STADIUM DEVELOPMENT, NW4

FOSTER & PARTNERS/HOK SPORT, 1994–

The existing (as of mid-2001) Wembley Stadium, a world-famous symbol of football and the venue for the annual Cup Final, was built in 1922–23 as one of the elements in the British Empire Exhibition of 1924. It was always, in fact, a multi-purpose venue and was used for athletic events at the 1948 London Olympics. By the early 1990s, the stadium was effectively worn-out and ill-equipped to compete for major international sporting events. It was probably the advent of the National Lottery, with its promise of funding, that stimulated plans for redevelopment. The project was seen as a potentially huge weapon for regeneration in the borough of Brent, one of London's poorest, with above-average unemployment.

Foster & Partners were first asked to draw up a scheme in 1994, when Wembley was competing against other cities, notably Manchester (which had bid for the Olympics [unsuccessfully] and the Commonwealth Games [successfully], to be the site of what was described as "the national stadium". The rebuilding of the stadium, as an 80,000-seat venue, with a retractable roof and the twin towers retained, was linked to a masterplan for a 300-acre site. The Foster scheme assured the selection of Wembley over Manchester.

Since 1997 the Wembley project, with an alliance of Foster and HOK Sport as designers, has been driven forward by the Wembley National Stadium Company. Football is the key element in the scheme, with provision for athletics and a strong commercial (conference/hotel/office) element tacked on. Currently costed at £326,000,000 (for 90,000 seats – close to the cost of the widely praised Stade de France in Paris), Wembley became bogged down in politics in 1999–2000. Financial underwriting from the government, rather than Lottery money, is now seen as a vital adjunct to securing finance in the City.

Architecturally the new stadium will be a landmark visible from the City of London, and Foster's great arch will provide more than adequate compensation for the loss of the towers. The reconstruction of the adjacent Underground station will be a major spin-off of the scheme and substantial commercial development will generate jobs and investment in north-west London. The project promises Britain "the world's best stadium", capable of accommodating a wide range of sports. Rescuing it from a crippling impasse is a priority for the mayor of London and ministers in Tony Blair's second administration.

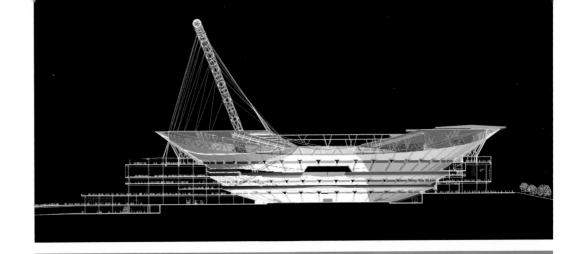

Opposite
The new stadium will offer world-class facilities for a wide range of sports

Right
Foster's dramatic arch will offer some compensation for the loss of the much-loved twin towers and will be a landmark across much of London, as seen here in a CAD image as viewed from Harrow on the Hill

ACAD CENTRE
CENTRAL MIDDLESEX HOSPITAL
PARK ROYAL, NW10

AVANTI ARCHITECTS, 1995–2000

The ACAD (ambulatory care and diagnostic) centre at Central Middlesex Hospital – once the Willesden Workhouse – is far removed, physically and in spirit, from the global concerns that are driving much of London's architectural scene. The 450-bed hospital serves a slice of north-west London that contains sizeable pockets of deprivation. Its setting, in a largely industrial landscape, is drab. Its buildings are utilitarian, at best, and ill-adapted to the needs of modern medicine. In short, Central Middlesex Hospital, though a well-respected institution, epitomizes the troubled image of Britain's National Health Service.

One new building that costs £12,500,000 cannot compensate for decades of underinvestment, yet Avanti's ACAD centre underlines the potent effect that a single inspirational structure can have on its surroundings and points the way towards continuing renewal of the site. The centre is designed for the diagnosis and treatment of ambulatory patients (those who do not require a hospital bed – there are no facilities in the building for overnight stays).

The triangular plan of the centre focuses on a central, nine-metre-high 'street', a generous, naturally lit space extending northwards from the spacious reception area (with its stylish coffee bar). West of the central spine is a two-storey treatment wing, with X-ray and other imaging facilities and operating theatres for minor surgery. To the east, consulting and treatment rooms are arranged around open, landscaped courts. The palette of materials for the building is necessarily economical – render, reconstituted stone and timber – but is used with a sure sense of style. Warm colours, judiciously applied, and crisp detailing help to banish memories of dreary NHS interiors. The response of patients and staff to this building has been enthusiastic – it is a tonic in its own right.

Right and opposite
The ACAD centre is a shot in the arm for a tired and dilapidated hospital campus, the stylish and colourful new building focusing on a daylit internal street

BRIXTON INTERMEDIATE CARE CENTRE
PULROSS ROAD, SW9
PENOYRE & PRASAD, 1999–2001

Despite the indisputable problems facing the National Health Service, the last decade has seen serious efforts to improve medical care in the community, with new medical centres established around London to provide a far wider range of services than that offered by the typical local general practitioner's surgery and providing an alternative to a conventional hospital for relatively straightforward treatments. The outcome has been commissions to a number of excellent architectural practices (Avanti, John Duane, Wharmby Kozdon and Pentarch, for example), but Penoyre & Prasad's centre at Rushton Street, Shoreditch (1997), was one of the best.

The same practice has recently completed the £2,300,000 care centre in Brixton, on part of the site of the old South Western Hospital. Penoyre & Prasad's vision is of an architecture that is not only functionally efficient, with up-to-date care facilities, but also welcoming and even therapeutic in character. From the street,

the building is prefaced by a terraced garden, with a glazed entrance façade connecting it to the surrounding neighbourhood. Inside, a café occupies part of the public space, with clinics and treatment rooms opening off it. Short-stay in-patient wards are on the first floor, overlooking a private garden to the rear as well as the public areas to the front. The aim is to offer patients a choice: involvement or privacy. The dining-room 'lantern' has a view down Pulross Road.

The architecture is pragmatic but elegant, with a mix of brickwork, render and timber on a concrete frame. The use of colour and natural timber is part of an agenda to provide a light and inspirational environment for patients and for those who work here. This is a building in the tradition of Berthold Lubetkin and Edward Cullinan (Penoyre & Prasad once worked for the latter) and is a positive contribution to the community in many respects.

Left and opposite
The transparent appearance of the centre opens up the building to the local community, and as such is the antithesis of the perceived image of National Health Service architecture

CHARTER SCHOOL, RED POST HILL, SE21

PENOYRE & PRASAD, 1999–2002

"Education, education, education": one of the key themes of the Blair government, which has expressed a determination to address the problem of under-achieving pupils and under-achieving schools. Clearly, wholesale demolition of failing schools is not a practical option. Penoyre & Prasad's makeover of the old premises of Dulwich High School for Boys (formerly William Penn School) to house the new Charter School suggests an alternative approach. Phase I was completed in autumn 2000, and further phases are ongoing, with a final roll-call of 1500 pupils envisaged by 2006.

The Charter School is a new comprehensive serving local children (who were previously obliged to attend schools across the borough) from a diverse social background, and it had hardly opened (in September 2000) before its first 180 places were oversubscribed by 500%. The bold and colourful new environment of the school has undoubtedly been part of the success story. One element in the formula was the creation of a real social heart with a sense of identity and community.

Penoyre & Prasad's raw material was a decent, if tired, campus of five detached buildings designed by LCC architects in the mid-1950s. The architecture had elegance, but it was austere and stranded in a bleak landscape. In terms of environmental performance, it did not meet modern standards. Its buildings were designed around an open courtyard – Penoyre & Prasad's key move was to roof over this space to create a covered atrium, an all-weather social forum, its roof supported on steel 'trees' painted green. The result is a solid, almost industrial aesthetic. The school is approached along a new landscaped 'boulevard' and entered at a single point, marked by a curving red wall, directly into the new atrium. The pedestrian route continues across the site connecting to new glazed routes between the buildings across landscaped courtyards. New lifts, strongly expressed within coloured shafts, provide access to levels for all pupils. Colour has been used boldly throughout. It is planned to reclad all the buildings in later phases of the project, with the reduction of energy and maintenance costs a clear objective. (The use of photovoltaic collectors is envisaged.) Although the architects tackled only two blocks, refurbishment of other blocks and the construction of further glazed routes is also planned.

This is a fine example of architectural transformation, achieved within public spending guidelines and with respect for the existing architectural context. The incisiveness of Penoyre & Prasad's approach, however, reflects the determination of all involved to create an outstanding new school. It is encouraging to see a practice of this calibre developing its portfolio of public commissions.

Left and opposite
At Charter School, Penoyre & Prasad have revitalized a worn-out campus of 1950s buildings, providing covered links and a new central atrium, its roof supported on rugged steel 'trees'

ELLIPSE BUILDING, ROYAL COLLEGE OF ART
KENSINGTON GORE, SW7

NICHOLAS GRIMSHAW & PARTNERS, 2000–2004

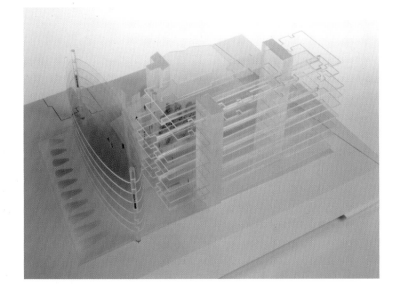

Grimshaw was selected as the architect for the Royal College of Art's new building in May 2000. The functional brief is demanding: 3000 square metres of new space housing studios, research facilities and a new gallery with the overall intention of fostering closer links between departments of fine art, applied art and design to encouraging dialogue and innovation. An equal challenge is provided by the setting – a site overlooking Kensington Gardens, yards from the Grade I listed Royal Albert Hall, with the new building forming a five-storey extension to the RCA's main Darwin building, a powerfully modelled but extremely urbane exercise in grainy concrete designed by Hugh Casson, Jim Cadbury-Brown and Robert Gooden.

The curved form of the new building, the 'Ellipse' as it has come to be known, is a clear nod to the Albert Hall but, combined with a mix of materials likely to focus on metal and glass, is also intended to provide a strong contrast to the rectangular geometry and solidity of the 1960s block.

The new building wraps around the west end of the Darwin building, which remains dominant. A new entrance to the college is provided on Kensington Gore, with a glazed reception area looking across to the park. Behind, a new vertical circulation core – "the mixing valve", as Grimshaw describes it – connects all floors of the two buildings, with a clear route through to the College's other accommodation along Jay Mews to the east. It will be a dramatic space, a focus for the RCA community. The structural strategy, developed with engineers Buro Happold, is intended to create uninterrupted, flexible spaces, generously daylit, while the servicing agenda is essentially low-energy, focusing on natural light and ventilation.

Grimshaw might not have seemed the obvious choice for this job: Will Alsop, for example, was another contender. Yet Grimshaw's highly practical addition is both elegant and sufficiently unassertive to win support from planners and other interested parties – or so one hopes.

GIRL GUIDES HEADQUARTERS
SOUTH WIMBLEDON, SW19

HUGH BROUGHTON ARCHITECTS, 1999–2000

The total cost of Hugh Broughton's elegant but robust headquarters for the South Wimbledon District Girl Guides (membership: two hundred and rising) was £189,916. The building is at the other end of the scale from many of the major public projects of the recent past, supported, as was this project, by Lottery grants. Yet its significance is all the greater: an inconspicuous building in an obscure suburb could easily have been a purely functional amenity. Broughton's building is a delight.

The guides previously used a former army hut, which steadily became unusable, on a landlocked site amid suburban streets. The brief to the architects was to design a new hall that could be let to other local groups, with kitchen, lavatories, committee room and store, all accessible to the disabled. Low maintenance and running costs were vital.

The completed building is straightforward: a steel-framed rectangle, largely glazed on the south front (which faces an open green space) on a brick base, with untreated cedar also used as a facing material. The monopitch roof, supported on slender trusses, is of corrugated steel.

Designing for children is a challenge: condescension comes easily. There is nothing twee or juvenile about this building, but it is designed with its users in mind. A long timber bench along the garden front, for example, comes in useful for out-of-door activities. Cedar *brise-soleils* guard against excessive solar gain.

The Lottery charities board gave £158,560 for this project: the remaining £40,000 was raised by the guides.

Key

1 Hall
2 Kitchen
3 Store
4 Committee Room

South Wimbledon District Guides Headquarters
Ground Floor Plan

Hugh Broughton Architects

Above and opposite
The Girl Guides centre in South Wimbledon is an example of a stylish but highly practical building designed and built to a tight budget and making good use of simple materials

HAMMERSMITH HEALTH CENTRE, W6

GUY GREENFIELD ARCHITECTS, 1996–2000

The centre of Hammersmith has never recovered from two disasters: the construction of the monstrous, polluting flyover and associated road links in the 1960s (would it have happened in Belgravia?) and the abandonment of Norman Foster's visionary transport interchange project (1977–80). It is now dominated by a dreary Post-modernist shopping and office centre, some packing case hotels and, of course, the flyover. The large, dull Victorian church of St Paul makes little impact in this context, though its immediate setting has been much improved in recent years by the creation of a small but pleasant park, and some efforts have been made, very belatedly, to tame the traffic and give pedestrians some rights. For all that, it is a dire spot.

Guy Greenfield's health centre, white and curvy, and with real value for the local community, is therefore a tonic for Hammersmith. It stands close to the church, on a busy traffic roundabout, hence the lack of windows on the street front. The architects were appointed in 1996 by the local health authority, and the building houses a large and busy medical group practice.

The eye-catching form of the centre is not merely arbitrary, but is designed to respond to the landscape of the new park and to baffle noise from the road. Inside, a corridor forms an additional barrier between the exterior and the medical consulting rooms, giving passers-by an oblique glimpse into the building across planted areas. A generous entrance area, further filtering the grime of the streets, leads to the reception lobby. A strong emphasis has been laid on clarity and legibility. Views out to the internal courtyard, with its Japanese-style garden, have a calming effect. The use of colour and natural materials – slate floors, for example, in public areas – is equally cheering. The project is rooted in a belief that surroundings matter to patients – a lesson that could be lost as the NHS pursues the course of Private Funding Initiative financing in the name of value for money.

JIGSAW DAY NURSERY, WANDSWORTH, SW18

WALTERS & COHEN, 2000–2001

Founded in 1994 by Cindy Walters and Michal Cohen, Walters & Cohen has acquired a reputation for fastidious detailing, an inspired use of materials and the ability to achieve wonders on modest budgets. Like many other young practices, it has lived to some extent on commissions for private houses and office fit-outs. Its abilities have come to the fore, however, in a series of nursery schools designed for Jigsaw Day Nurseries plc, a company that has successfully capitalized on the demand, largely from young professionals, for high-quality childcare. The first project for Jigsaw, in Bristol, was completed in 1997, with a second scheme, at Stockley

Park, near Heathrow, following a year later; both schemes successfully overcame the potential hurdle of design-and-build contracts.

The Wandsworth nursery is very different, in that it is not a new building but a fit-out of space in a relatively run-of-the-mill luxury housing development close to Wandsworth Bridge. It fits easily into a run of shops and restaurants. The nursery facilities are housed in a series of pods – flexible spaces that can be opened up or enclosed as the activities in hand demand. The double-height space in which they sit provided scope for a mezzanine retreat for staff. A garden, designed by the architects,

is a natural extension of the internal space: the opportunity to play in the fresh air is seen as an important asset. One of the most striking features of the project is the extensive use of natural materials: the birch-faced ply, for example, used to clad the pods, and the timber furniture. On one level, the nursery provides a natural environment for the privileged youngsters who will be the trend-setters of the 2020s. But it also offers a model for nursery provision more generally: its avoidance of the clichés of 'child-centred' design is very welcome.

Below and opposite
The nursery, housed in an unremarkable commercial development, demonstrates a clever use of scale and natural materials, providing a friendly environment for children

PRIMARY SCHOOL AND HEALTH CENTRE GREENWICH MILLENNIUM VILLAGE, SE10

EDWARD CULLINAN ARCHITECTS, 1998–2001

Another project from a long-established practice that still designs with the enthusiasm of youth. The brief for the project was strongly practical – a school for 420 children, aged four to eleven, with provisions for those with special educational needs and facilities for the extended local community in a large attached hall, and a well-equipped district health centre – and highly innovative. The inter-connected buildings address the ambitious agenda for new sustainable urban communities, developed on brownfield sites, set out in the 1999 Urban Task Force report. They equally reflect new ideas of integrating educational, health and other community services in complexes that provide the urban villages of the future with a recognizable public focus.

The site is at the north-west entrance to the Millennium Village, on the pedestrian route to the Dome; the circular hall is seen as a gatepost to the residential development. The buildings are arranged around and entered from a piazza, with the more private classrooms and consulting and treatment rooms facing south into enclosed gardens and play areas. Extensive shading protects these spaces from direct sunlight in summer. The use of an innovative passive cooling system ensures comfortable conditions, while high levels of insulation cut winter heating bills. Materials are conspicuously natural – lots of timber on a steel frame – and used in a straightforward Cullinan way, without recourse to mere folksiness. The walls of English larch enclosing the piazza are reassuring in the, as yet, bleak landscape of the Greenwich peninsula, which is, within living memory, the site of Europe's largest gasworks.

The protracted controversy over the Dome has obscured the significance of the wider regeneration programme that is transforming the surrounding area. Cullinan's optimistic and cheerful architecture confounds the sceptics and points the way toward the rebirth of London's forgotten backyard.

Opposite, above and right
This development includes a range of community facilities forming a social focus for the new housing on the Greenwich peninsula, and makes use of a broad palette of largely natural materials

THE PRINCE'S FOUNDATION
CHARLOTTE ROAD, SHOREDITCH, EC2
MATTHEW LLOYD ARCHITECTS, 1998–2000

Matthew Lloyd's conversion of a former warehouse in the modish designer-land of Shoreditch might seem an incongruous base for an operation that carries the torch of the Prince of Wales's architectural and urban campaigns. A great deal has changed, however, since the prince waged war on modern architecture in the 1980s and took up the cause of literal Classicism at Paternoster Square and elsewhere. Advised to eschew political (including planning) issues, the prince directed his fire elsewhere, only to immerse himself in equally contentious issues like organic farming and genetic engineering.

The prince's interest in architecture, though apparently dominated by issues of style, was always linked to a vision of society, hence his interest in community and 'green' design. With the dissolution of his Institute of Architecture, based in polite Regent's Park, these issues have come to the fore in the curriculum of the new Prince's Foundation, with its strong connections to urban regeneration and conservation and broad teaching and research agenda. (Ominously, however, the prince's first speech delivered at the foundation reiterated some of his well-rehearsed charges against modernism.)

Matthew Lloyd's conversion project is respectful where it needs to be – the street façade, for example, has hardly been altered – and interventionist where the practical brief demands. Inside the front door, the first radical move – a brick ramp up to the reception area – is immediately visible. The second is the insertion of a steel staircase to connect all levels of the building, a focus for chance meetings as much as a means of circulation. From the staircase void there are views into the studios and other spaces. The impressive top-floor space contains a drawing studio and lecture room separated by a movable partition. Lloyd's most striking addition to the historic fabric is found at roof level, where two sculptural ventilation cowls, suitably industrial in appearance, signal the low-energy servicing strategy of the project.

The building represents a striking, even touching, gesture towards contemporary concerns that suggests that the prince's enterprise might genuinely have taken a new direction. It remains to be seen how much of the promise of Shoreditch is reflected in the foundation's work.

Right and opposite
The exterior of the warehouse building remains largely unchanged while interior spaces have been quite radically reconfigured, with a new steel staircase connecting all levels and providing interesting views into studios and other working areas

ROYAL ACADEMY OF MUSIC
MARYLEBONE ROAD, NW1

JOHN McASLAN & PARTNERS, 1998–2001

The Royal Academy of Music is England's oldest centre of musical training, founded in 1823 under the patronage of George IV. It moved to the Marylebone Road in 1912, to a new building designed by Sir Ernest George, with teaching rooms, offices and a concert hall, the Duke's Hall. The academy has had several phases of expansion since, including the radical conversion of a war-damaged Nash terrace on York Gate. McAslan's development scheme seeks to weld together the disparate elements of the institution to form an attractive central London campus.

The challenge of the site, a gap between listed buildings close to Regent's Park, was matched by that of the client brief, which called for new teaching and practice rooms, a museum to house the academy's remarkable collection of manuscripts and historic instruments, and a small concert hall capable of being used for recording sessions.

McAslan's solution has been to sink the concert hall, seating 175, into the site, from which it emerges as a long barrel-vaulted form. A new central square for the academy is formed around this intervention.

Right
The project provides for a new concert hall, seen under construction below, slotted in to the gap between the original building of 1912 and the converted terrace on York Gate

Opposite
The York Gate terrace has been radically refurbished to provide greatly improved rehearsal facilities

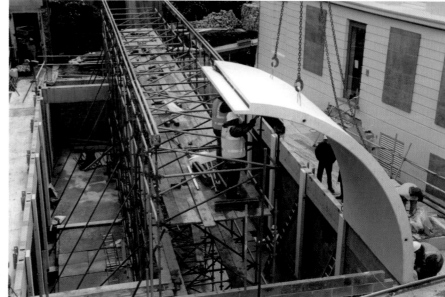

Below and opposite
The school makes good use of a constricted site,
providing sports facilities and other open spaces
alongside colourful and strongly modelled new
buildings

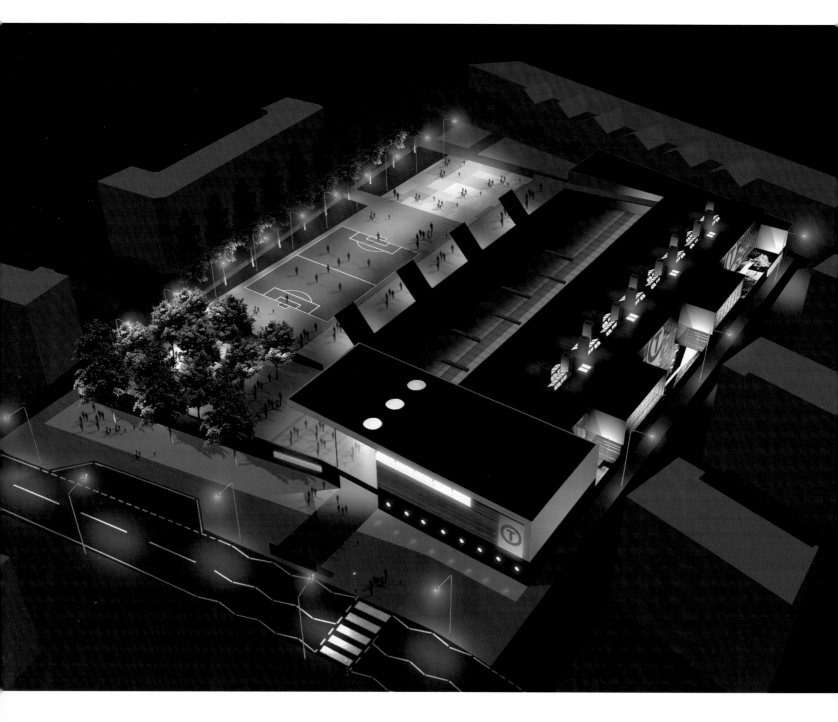

TULSE HILL SCHOOL, TULSE HILL, SW2
ALLFORD HALL MONAGHAN MORRIS, 2000–2002

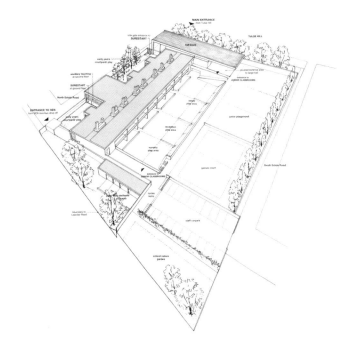

Allford Hall Monaghan Morris's new school at Great Notley, Essex, completed in 1999, is one of the most discussed educational buildings of recent years, not least for its sustainable services strategy, and reflects the expressive but highly analytical approach of this outstanding young firm. The commission at Tulse Hill was won in competition and provides a new school with 420 places, including nursery, primary and special needs provisions, on the site of the former Brockwell Primary School.

The site is far from large and the aim was to retain as much open space as possible for playgrounds and sports and to give the new school a green setting. The two-storey classroom block is placed along the northern edge of the site, with primary classes at first floor level, nursery classes on the ground level and all children entering through a common entrance on Tulse Hill. The school has a strong presence on the street. A blue-brick-clad wall marks its presence, with the timber-clad hall, intended for use by the wider community as well as the school, sitting on top, its roof oversailing to provide a sheltered space for outdoor activities.

This is colourful urban architecture, designed with children in mind and avoiding the segregation that used to isolate those with special needs, but also contributing to the life of a relatively disadvantaged inner-city community.

UNIVERSITY OF EAST LONDON DOCKLANDS CAMPUS, E16

EDWARD CULLINAN ARCHITECTS, 1997–99

Given the social conviction, humane pragmatism and youthful verve of its completed projects in the capital (beginning with Ted Cullinan's own marvellous low-budget house, completed in 1964), Edward Cullinan Architects has built far too little in London. The new campus for the University of East London in the Royal Docks is a visual delight, as it needs to be. The pace of development in the Royals has been slow, with the 1990s recession scuppering some major projects: a lack of adequate transport infrastructure, only partly addressed by the Docklands Light Railway, has been an obvious problem. Premature clearance of existing buildings, some with great potential for reuse, has created daunting expanses of emptiness. The first two decades of the new century, however, should see the Royals boom. Cullinan's campus may soon cease to be an outpost.

The site is alongside the Royal Albert Dock, close to the Dockland Light Railway's Cyprus station and facing London City Airport across the water. Locating an educational campus here was seen as a way of stimulating development, including investment in scientific research facilities, and twenty-eight start-up units were included in the scheme. The project was funded by an alliance of public and private interests and built to a tight budget on the basis of a 'develop-and-construct' contract, with details formulated by the contractor. The campus was built in eighteen months.

The brief was for a masterplan providing for a campus to accommodate 7000 students: the first phase was to accommodate 2400 in eight departments, with 384 residential places. The monumental scale of earlier buildings in the Royals was clearly unachievable: instead, Cullinan opted for strong form and vivid colour, plus a decisive landscape strategy, to create a sense of identity and place. The academic departments are arranged as a south facing 'cliff', with the residences arranged as free-standing four-storey drums, coloured green, yellow or blue, around a public square. The low-energy ventilation/heating system was developed (with engineers Whitby & Bird) in response to an environment where noise from the City Airport is a major issue.

This scheme demonstrates the potential of the newest universities to venture where older institutions would fear to tread. It also shows the skill of the architects to secure exemplary results with a procurement process that often produces banality. This is good, practical design for a classic 'brownfield' location, with a generous dose of delight thrown in.

HOUSING

ARSENAL FOOTBALL CLUB REDEVELOPMENT
ALLIES & MORRISON

COOKSON SMITH HOUSE, TWICKENHAM
EDWARD CULLINAN ARCHITECTS

ECO-TOWER, ELEPHANT & CASTLE
KEN YEANG/HTA ARCHITECTS LTD.

ELEKTRA HOUSE, WHITECHAPEL
ADJAYE & ASSOCIATES

GAINSBOROUGH STUDIOS, POOLE STREET
MUNKENBECK & MARSHALL

HOUSE, 125 GOLDEN LANE
USE ARCHITECTS (JO HAGAN)

HOUSE, 180 HIGHBURY HILL
CHARLES THOMSON/RIVINGTON STREET STUDIO

HOUSE, TITE STREET
TONY FRETTON ARCHITECTS

HOUSING, COIN STREET
HAWORTH TOMPKINS ARCHITECTS

HOUSING/HOSTEL, HACKNEY ROAD
FRASER BROWN MacKENNA

KEELING HOUSE REFURBISHMENT, CLAREDALE STREET
MUNKENBECK & MARSHALL

LONDON TOWN: 44 HOPTON STREET
KEVIN DASH ARCHITECTS/GAMUCHDJIAN ASSOCIATES

LOTS ROAD POWER STATION
TERRY FARRELL & PARTNERS

MILLENNIUM VILLAGE HOUSING, GREENWICH
PROCTOR MATTHEWS ARCHITECTS

PEABODY HOUSING, MURRAY GROVE
CARTWRIGHT PICKARD ARCHITECTS

PRIORY HEIGHTS, PRIORY GREEN ESTATE
AVANTI ARCHITECTS

10–22 SHEPHERDESS WALK
BUSCHOW HENLEY

THE SKYHOUSE
MARKS BARFIELD ARCHITECTS

STRAW HOUSE AND QUILTED OFFICE, STOCK ORCHARD STREET
SARAH WIGGLESWORTH ARCHITECTS/JEREMY TILL

ARSENAL FOOTBALL CLUB REDEVELOPMENT
AVENELL ROAD, N5

ALLIES & MORRISON, 2000–06

Arsenal Football Club's (not uncontentious) decision to relocate its ground to Ashburton Grove, some distance from the existing Highbury stadium, with a new £300,000,000, state-of-the-art stadium designed by HOK Sport, posed the question of what could be done with the stands at Highbury, one of which (the Avenell Road east stand) is listed.

Early in 2000 Allies & Morrison was asked to produce proposals for the reuse of the Highbury site, with the emphasis on residential development. The idea of converting a football ground to a new residential quarter is entirely novel, yet the proposed solution seems completely rational and could produce something unique. The east and west stands are to be converted into residential space, with highly transparent, curtain-walled elevations overlooking the former pitch area, which is to be relandscaped as a series of enclosed gardens, with a car park at basement level. The overhanging stand roofs provide a

convenient means of shading these elevations. Inside the stands, existing foyer areas are to be retained as entrances to the blocks. The present north and south stands, which are of no special interest, are to be demolished and replaced by new residential blocks, smaller in scale than the retained stands but sufficiently tall to retain the sense of enclosure that is a prime characteristic of the ground. Double-height living spaces are intended to make maximum use of the attractive setting.

It is proposed to create an improved route into the site from Arsenal station, with a low-rise development of mews-style houses, plus some light industrial space, a token nod, perhaps, to the prescription for mixed-use development. The inclusion of a significant quantity of affordable housing is a welcome and necessary ingredient in what is a highly commercial development, intended to underwrite the club's investment in a new venue for Premier League football.

Right and opposite
As part of the proposal to convert Arsenal's famous ground to residential use, two of the former stands will become apartment buildings, while the pitch will be transformed into a series of enclosed gardens, with car parking beneath

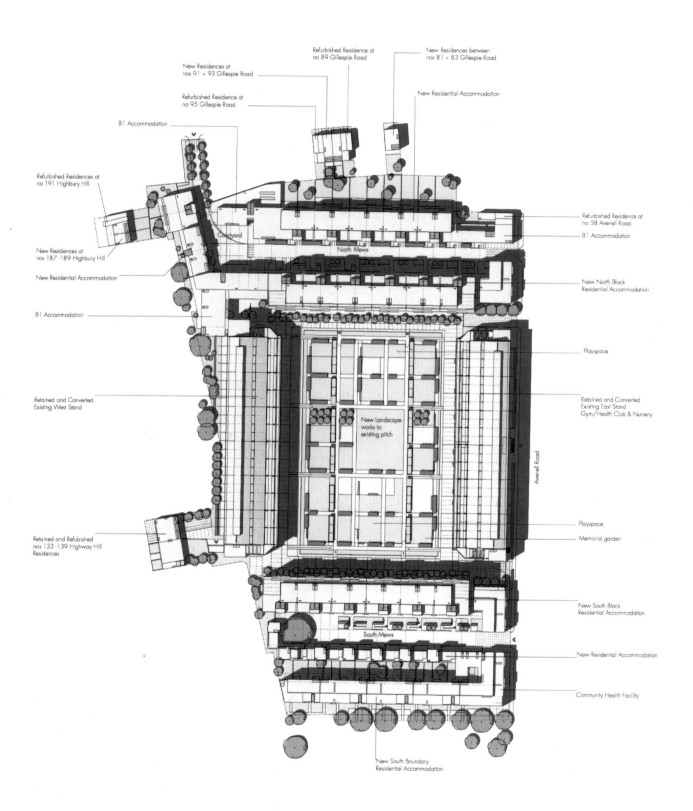

New Residences at
nos 91 + 93 Gillespie Road

Refurbished Residence at
no 89 Gillespie Road

New Residences between
nos 81 + 83 Gillespie Road

Refurbished Residence at
no 95 Gillespie Road

New Residential Accommodation

B1 Accommodation

Refurbished Residences at
no 191 Highbury Hill

Refurbished Residence at
no 58 Avenell Road

B1 Accommodation

Courtyard

North Mews

New Residences at
nos 187 -189 Highbury Hill

New Residential Accommodation

New North Block
Residential Accommodation

B1 Accommodation

Playspace

Retained and Converted
Existing West Stand

Retained and Converted
Existing East Stand
Gym/Health Club & Nursery

New Landscape
works to
existing pitch

Avenell Road

Playspace

Retained and Refurbished
nos 133 -139 Highway Hill
Residences

Memorial garden

New South Block
Residential Accommodation

South Mews

New Residential Accommodation

Community Health Facility

New South Boundary
Residential Accommodation

COOKSON SMITH HOUSE, TWICKENHAM
EDWARD CULLINAN ARCHITECTS, 1999–2000

Opposite
Skilful use has been made of a relatively narrow site, with stepped pavilions extending from road to riverbank

Below
Externally faced in natural materials – in particular brick and timber – the house has a spectacular internal living space that looks out on to the river

The Cullinan office has designed remarkably few private houses, unsurprisingly, perhaps, given its strong commitment to social and public architecture. The exceptions are the houses built by the members of the practice for themselves, including Ted Cullinan's own residence, self-built "during two years of Sundays between 1962 and 1964". The architect for whom this luxurious riverside pavilion was designed presumably has neither the time nor the inclination for self-building.

The key issue was clearly the relationship of the house to the river. The architects' first inclination was to capitalize on it by creating a series of pavilions along the full width of the plot, but this proposal foundered after planners insisted on a rigorous programme of tree preservation (mere sycamores, it should be said). Instead, the house assumed a superficially straightforward rectangular form; even so, a planning appeal was needed before consent was given. In fact, the block is still broken down into three linked pavilions arranged on a north–south axis, two of three storeys, one of two storeys, under gently curving roofs, oversailing at the edges. A similar treatment is applied to the detached garage (with service flat above) on the road front of the site, so that the rhythm of curves extends across the whole complex of structures, marking a progression from road to river, from public to private domain. A timber deck extends through the entrance lobby (covered by a curved canopy) right down to the river bank, terminating in what looks like a diving board.

The use of brick and red cedar as the principal facing materials allows the house to fit easily into the local scene. The interior contains some surprises: a great full-height curving wall runs right through it, linking the spaces. It is punctuated by a series of openings and niches, elements in the rich texture of a house that the critic Jonathan Hale thought "more John Soane than John Pawson – and, I imagine, all the more liveable for it".

ECO-TOWER, ELEPHANT & CASTLE, SE1

KEN YEANG/HTA ARCHITECTS LTD, 2002–

Malaysian architect Ken Yeang, who trained at the Architecture Association in London (where he was influenced by Archigram and Cedric Price), has devoted his career to addressing environmental issues in the context of modern design. He can be regarded as the pioneer of the 'green skyscraper', stating that his interest is "the holistic consideration of the sustainable use of energy and materials over the life-cycle of a building 'system', from source of materials to their inevitable disposal and/or subsequent recycling".

Yeang was brought into the design team at Elephant & Castle by HTA, a London practice that has transformed many worn-out local authority high-rises into attractive modern residential spaces. The masterplan for the area envisages a strong emphasis on sustainability: the Eco-Tower demonstrates that sustainable housing can be architecturally dramatic and developed on high-rise principles.

The tower (forty storeys, 150 metres high) is a world away from earlier high-rise housing blocks in Britain. It allows for secure and convenient living close to the heart of London and is designed to encourage the development of new urban communities that will live harmoniously and in surroundings that are 'greened' by the use of balconies, private gardens, and communal 'sky gardens'. The apartments are designed as flexible and adaptable spaces, catering to a wide range of households; they are naturally lit and ventilated and located on top of developing public transport facilities. The design of the tower is calculated to control the effects of wind to ensure comfortable climates at all levels. Solar energy systems are to be extensively utilized. At the lower levels of the tower, the public will have access to retail and community facilities.

The ideal is that of an environmentally aware, sustainable, mixed community that contributes to the regeneration and economic revival of the area. With the right funding base, towers of this kind – and the aim is to build a number of them around London – could become practical demonstrations of the principles of Richard Rogers's Urban Task Force report.

Right
The Eco-Tower makes innovative use of balconies, private green spaces and communal 'sky gardens' as part of a progressive agenda for low-energy high-rise housing in the inner city

ELEKTRA HOUSE, WHITECHAPEL, E1
ADJAYE & ASSOCIATES, 1999–2000

Below
If the street façade, clad in black resin-coated plywood panels, is regarded by some as perversely blank, the rear is altogether lighter in tone and heavily glazed, offering views on to a small courtyard garden

This is one of the most sensational new houses in London, a building that has the same power to shock and to annoy as the work of some of the artists for whom Adjaye, a new-generation star, has designed homes and studios. Its publication in an architectural journal produced much splenetic comment. Not the least of the charges laid against it was that its response to the street was hostile, defensive and anti-social, while exception was taken to its use as a family home.

Two artists were the clients for the Elektra House, located in a gritty but fashionable quarter of the East End. The decision to light the house entirely from above and from the rear, courtyard elevation was partly practical (for security and to obtain large interior wall surfaces for displaying art works) and partly the arbitrary decision of a designer who likes to do the unexpected. The street façade is clad in panels of black resin-coated plywood and is uncompromised by any openings; the entrance is *via* a passage to the side. Inside, the house is painted all white. The ground floor is almost entirely taken up by a studio/living room that opens into a small walled yard. A double-height slot illuminates the space and the staircase. The first floor contains three bedrooms and a bathroom, all largely dependent on roof lights for illumination and uncommonly tall in proportion.

This is an uncompromising statement of a house, tailor-made for the lifestyle of a particular family. Neither the street in which it stands nor London has been impoverished by it. Rather the opposite: it is a statement about the right of architect and client to work together to create something remarkable; London is being wrecked by house builders who create a standard product without reference to future users. In case the Elektra House should be considered an extravagant project, its cost should be put on record: £80,000 for 130 square metres of space, exclusive of site and fees.

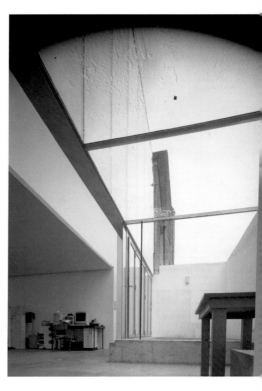

MUNKENBECK & MARSHALL, 2001–02

Opposite and below
The Gainsborough Studios project combines
refurbishment and rebuild and mixes uses,
including housing, offices, design studios
and galleries, in a way that typifies the best
regeneration projects of the present day

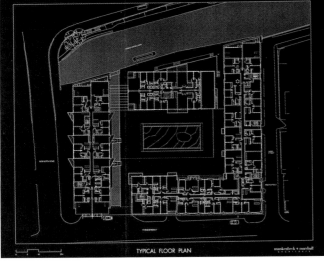

TYPICAL FLOOR PLAN

Unearthing a still-undeveloped site of this quality in the Islington/Shoreditch hinterland is something of an achievement in itself, but Munkenbeck & Marshall's approach to Gainsborough Studios looks set to turn the complex into a model mixed-use, new/old city community.

The existing building that forms the core of the development has already gone through several changes of use. It was constructed as a power station, with London's third tallest chimney, which was demolished, alas, in 1940 as a potential marker for Nazi bombers. Between the wars it housed the famous Gainsborough Studios, a powerhouse of the fledgling British film industry. Hitchcock filmed here on many occasions as the big, tough power station could house any scenario (it could be flooded for naval movies). After the Second World War, the site degenerated into light industrial use and planning consent was obtained to flatten it. Developer Keith Meehan of Lincoln Holdings saw the potential for a more imaginative approach and responded to pleas from prominent film industry figures, including Lord Attenborough, to retain the historic studio block.

Film and photographic studios, offices for media companies, an art gallery and restaurants will be housed in the converted building, with apartments on upper floors. The new blocks respond to their location close to the Grand Union Canal: they are laid around a new square and canalside walk and feature nautical-looking balconies and ship-lapped timber boarding as cladding. The conservation and mixed-use aspects of the project appealed to the local authority, which allowed a much more dense development than that originally approved – the tallest of the new blocks, at the corner of New North Road, rises to fourteen storeys. This block, with its striking steel fins, is seen as a marker for the site when approached from the City. Within the site, a giant head of Alfred Hitchcock – big enough to house an editing suite – will be an equally notable landmark. The scheme will include 176 apartments (40 built for a housing association) and 77 live/work units.

HOUSE, 125 GOLDEN LANE, EC1

USE ARCHITECTS (JO HAGAN), 1999–2000

An oddity and a gem: a house just 3.5 metres wide slotted into the densely developed urban fabric of Clerkenwell and making a distinctive contribution to a townscape that includes Chamberlin, Powell & Bon's Golden Lane Estate and the spectacular towers of the same firm's Barbican development.

Hagan acquired the site when it housed nothing more than a shed, used by a mini-cab firm, squeezed into the gap between a Victorian commercial block and a pub. He intended to build a house for himself but ended up completing the project for a client, a couple with a young child. Negotiating with adjacent owners was one of the hardest parts of the project: inserting 13-metre piles meant working next to party walls. The plan emerges from the site: there was space for just one room per floor. The house has five floors, plus a basement and a small top floor space in a set-back behind

a roof terrace. The client's decision that a lift was a vital addition to the original proposals further restricted the internal space. The lift was inserted as a concrete shaft into a lightweight, steel-framed structure and is seen as a freestanding object. To the street, the house is a sheer composition of steel and glass, like a fragment of some large Mies tower, and the detailing is sufficiently precise to bear out the illusion. On the exposed side wall, timber cladding has been used, with a cut-out to allow views from the roof.

Five-storey houses are common enough in London, a vertical city. In many Georgian houses, staircases form the *tour de force,* and Hagan has worked within this tradition, making the stair a huge lightwell with views both inwards and outwards. The total cost of the project was £425,000 – reasonable for a house that is likely to remain a one-off.

Right and opposite
Highly vertical in the London tradition, and a rare example of an entirely new house close to the centre of the City, this project makes daring use of an alarmingly narrow site

HOUSE, 180 HIGHBURY HILL, N5

CHARLES THOMSON/RIVINGTON STREET STUDIO, 1999–2000

Close to Arsenal's Highbury ground and Arsenal tube station, in an area of modest Victorian terraced houses, a new house utilizes a typical piece of urban waste ground formerly occupied by a derelict workshop. The aim was to design a classic modern house without concessions to history but in sympathy with the neighbourhood – 'modern, but contextual' is the formula. The relationship of the new building to the street and the way in which its response to the public domain was balanced by issues of seclusion and

privacy were part of a dialogue with planners.

On the street front, the house maintains the two-storey scale of its neighbours, rising to three storeys at the rear. The designs seek to reinterpret the traditional formula of the London terraced house in a contemporary way. The roof is of zinc, rather than slate or tiles, the walls are white, sealed with an acrylic finish that eliminates the need for cavities and internal insulation. The steel-framed windows are slim and precise and adapted in form to their

location: large bay windows on the street provide generous light and views out; on the rear elevation, long horizontal windows are more modern.

The plan is far from traditional, with a large L-shaped living room as the principal space, opening on to a garden deck. A further living/dining space occupies much of the first floor. Ceiling heights throughout are uncommonly generous by modern standards; indeed, the dimensions feel Victorian rather than modern.

Opposite
This house is uncompromisingly modern while respectful of its Victorian neighbours

Right and below
Inside, the use of light is modulated through narrow fenestration, while the aesthetic is modernist in its restraint

HOUSE, TITE STREET, SW3

TONY FRETTON ARCHITECTS, 1997–2001

Tony Fretton's Lisson Gallery, in Lisson Street, Marylebone, completed a decade ago, was a radical statement about the nature of an art gallery, in spatial and in urban terms: the Lisson is a gallery on the street, open in its nature, with apartments above the display spaces.

Fretton's Chelsea house, designed for a reclusive art collector, is equally an urban statement, imbued with the architect's subtle and austere approach to space and form. The context is a street where the dominant theme is the late Victorian Domestic Revival style: red brick, bays and bows, all 'sweetness and light' – potentially dangerous territory for anyone trying to build in a contemporary way. In this instance, Fretton needed all the subtlety at his command to overcome possible objections, yet the house, though a private domain, is anything but recessive or anonymous. Its street front, indeed, has a solid dignity that Fretton sees as "civic – like a Venetian palazzo. Contributing to the city without being open to the public." The comparison is borne out by the plan of the house, with a grand saloon at first

floor (*piano nobile*), extending into a void on the second floor, where there is a library. The spaces on these floors are intended for entertaining and the display of works of art. More mundane activities are conducted on the first and third floors and in the basement. The house includes a small enclosed garden at the rear. It is, of course, an artistic house in the best Chelsea tradition: one recalls Whistler's house in Tite Street, designed by E.W. Godwin and proto-modern in its austerity.

Godwin's protest against convention lay in the use of white paint. Fretton is more contextual: the red limestone (an opulent choice of material) in which the house is clad is hardly an outrage in a street of red brick. But the precision with which it is used is more Miesian than Arts and Crafts. The house could be seen as over-monumental – a display of wealth – and defensive. But Fretton's references to Renaissance palazzi make sense. This house enriches the street. What goes on inside is the business of the owner – but one longs to see the interiors.

Right
The rigour and monumentality of this house provide a sensitive contrast with the more ornamental façades of its largely Victorian neighbours

The generous scale of the house is equally reflected in the interiors, intended for the display of artworks

Opposite
At the rear, a small enclosed garden can be enjoyed as much from inside as out

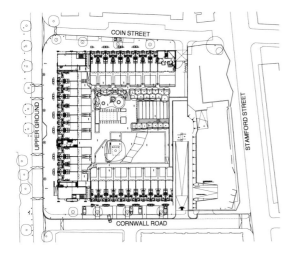

HOUSING, COIN STREET, SE1

HAWORTH TOMPKINS ARCHITECTS, 1997–2001

This development of fifty-nine dwellings, including thirty-two family houses, by one of London's most dynamic young practices forms the latest segment in Coin Street Community Builders' ongoing development of the fourteen acres of land it acquired from the GLC in 1984 (purchase price: £1,000,000). The memory of the earliest work here – uninspired and suburban in character – has now been laid to rest as Coin Street moves on from the excellent mid-1990s contribution by Lifschutz Davidson (twenty-five units, including a nine-storey block) to this latest phase. Fifteen years ago innovative design and social conviction seemed to be at odds, but this is no longer the case in Livingstone's London.

Haworth Tompkins won the commission in 1997. The site, formerly occupied by warehousing but used for surface parking for many years, is close to the National Theatre and high-rise IBM headquarters. The character of the new housing is suitably urban, mediating between the cultural/public territory of the South Bank and the modest residential streets beyond. There are four-storey houses on Coin Street and Cornwall Road. On Upper Ground, a busy public route through the area, the scale is even bigger, with two-storey

maisonettes squatting on top of three-storey houses. Doors are on the street and houses have private gardens. Both the scale and the layout of the scheme (around a central square, with parking underneath) look back to Georgian tradition, though there is nothing overtly historicist about the architecture. On the street façades, a disciplined and impervious brick cladding is used. On the courtyard side, steel-and-timber balconies, with trellises and louvred-timber sun shades, create a softer, more lively and informal look. The materials have been used with a view to energy conservation. High levels of insulation and roof-mounted solar panels will make the dwellings economical to run – this is sustainability in action.

The fourth side of the central square is to be occupied by the Hothouse, a new training centre with an IT resource centre, conference and classrooms, exhibition spaces, social facilities and small offices for local arts and community organizations. Facing the heavily trafficked Stamford Street, the building will provide a powerful image of genuinely creative community action to generate homes, employment and regeneration in partnership with business and government.

Opposite and top
The scheme proposes a new residential square – a modern interpretation of an old London tradition

Above
Faced in brick to the surrounding streets, the housing blocks are more informal in appearance on the elevations overlooking the new square, and balconies, trellises and sunshading create a lively aesthetic

HOUSING/HOSTEL, HACKNEY ROAD, E2

FRASER BROWN MacKENNA, 1998–2000

Over the last few decades, housing associations have served London well not only by providing thousands of houses and flats at reasonable rents but equally by building in locations that, until recently, commercial developers would not touch, and by promoting urban repair by infilling often small and awkward derelict sites. This approach, in tune with the recommendations of the Urban Task Force, contrasts with the total clearance campaigns of local authorities in the 1950s and 1960s and has produced excellent work by practices such as Hunt Thompson, Avanti, Pollard Thomas Edwards and Levitt

Bernstein. Current government policies place the associations at the fore of efforts to provide 'social' and affordable housing in inner London, and the dynamic approach to commissioning and design pursued by organizations like the Peabody Trust shows that they are up to the challenge. Peabody, in particular, has had the courage to commission housing from a number of young practices.

The scheme at Hackney Road was developed by Peabody for occupation by the Providence Row housing association, an East End-based charity that aims to provide a 'bridge' for long-term homeless

and street sleepers working towards a home of their own.

The site contained derelict shops fronting a yard filled with single-storey sheds. The development retains the street line on Hackney Road, with two new lettable shops to replace those demolished. The brief was to create a friendly and welcoming environment, but one where residents would be reassured by a degree of security. There is a ten-bed hostel for short-term residents and twenty-five furnished self-contained flats. The sole entry point is off Hackney Road, where a slatted-timber ramp connects the street to

an entrance courtyard. The flats, approached by a second ramp, are arranged around a quiet central court. At the rear of the site, they are configured to suggest a traditional East End terrace: daylit staircases provide an attractive alternative to institutional corridors. The mix of materials – cedar, stock brick, powder-coated steel and glass – is contemporary and used with a view to hard wear and low maintenance.

This is 'social' architecture for today: appealing to look at and with no hints of condescension, yet achieved at moderate cost and enhancing its context.

KEELING HOUSE REFURBISHMENT
CLAREDALE STREET, E2
MUNKENBECK & MARSHALL, 1999–2001

Munkenbeck & Marshall's revamp of Keeling House, Bethnal Green, as luxury apartments was welcomed by the original architect of the sixteen-storey block of maisonettes, the late Sir Denys Lasdun, though the project was at odds with the intentions behind his design. Built in 1957–59 for the borough council, Keeling House, like the slightly earlier 'cluster blocks' in Usk Street, represented a sincere attempt to create an environment where the community spirit of the East End might live on, even after the demolition of the traditional terraced streets of the area. The balconies, for example, were intended to encourage neighbourly chats.

Keeling House was emptied of tenants in 1992, when its allegedly poor structural condition began to give cause for alarm. Efforts to fund a refurbishment by a housing association failed and in 1999 the building, by then utterly derelict, was sold to a private developer. Saved from possible demolition by Grade II* listing, it had acquired the status of a modern classic.

The refurbishment project highlighted the relatively sound condition of the block: the concrete, in generally good condition, was sealed with a new protective coating. Original colours were reinstated throughout. In tune with the expectations of the new owner-occupiers, the setting of the building was enhanced and landscaped, with extensive planting and a pool within a secure enclosure. Lasdun and his former partner John Hurley collaborated on the design of a new entrance lobby, its triangular geometry derived from the form of the building.

Lasdun, who felt that gentrification was preferable to demolition, was equally supportive of a proposal to build a new penthouse on top of the block, but this was vetoed after a public inquiry in 2001, when a tablet in his memory was unveiled in the entrance lobby.

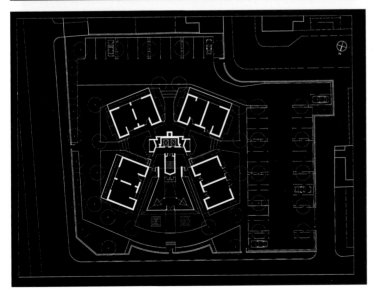

Opposite
A new entrance lobby was added to the existing building as part of its conversion

Left
The form of Sir Denys Lasdun's original cluster blocks has adapted well to the lifestyle of a social group far removed from the original inhabitants of the scheme

The development includes new landscaping of the area around the building, and secure car parking

LONDON TOWN: 44 HOPTON STREET, SE1

KEVIN DASH ARCHITECTS/GUMUCHDJIAN ASSOCIATES,
1999–

The Cesar Pelli-designed residential tower adjacent to the Museum of Modern Art, New York, is one of the most desirable addresses in Manhattan. Now London could have its own version of the MOMA tower, with nearly half of the units allocated to affordable housing for the key workers – doctors, nurses, teachers and the like – who are marginalized by London's booming housing market. Kevin Dash and Philip Gumuchdjian's scheme, designed for developer London Town plc, has, not surprisingly, attracted the support of Mayor Livingstone, whose vision of a booming capitalist economy fuelling social progress it so vividly reflects.

The site is that of a paper warehouse, a pathetic, if unsightly, survival of the industries that once dominated the Bankside area. Close to Tate Modern, it is an incongruous relic and forms an impenetrable obstacle to the large numbers of visitors flowing into the Tate from Southwark station and Blackfriars Bridge. In contrast, the proposed thirty-three-storey, 107-metre tower (a little higher than the Tate's chimney stack) has a relatively small footprint – half the site – and opens up new perspectives of and routes to Britain's most visited art gallery. The development is in tune with the Richard Rogers Partnership masterplan for the future development of the environs of Tate Modern. The slender form of the tower is doubly important, first, in visual terms, in eschewing any challenge to Giles Scott's

brick colossus, and secondly, more practically, in avoiding significant shadowing of adjacent housing and minimizing wind turbulence.

The thirty-three apartments vary in size – the grandest are two-storey penthouses, commanding some of the best views in London and likely to command record prices. Yet the project has a serious environmental, as well as social, agenda. Its highly glazed form is mediated by the use of timber louvres (on south and south-west façades) and automated sunshading. The use of chilled soffits, rather than conventional air-conditioning, to assist cooling is another progressive move. A layer of double-height winter gardens

provides insulation against the fickle London climate and introduces an element of delight into the residential spaces. In fine weather, open terraces and balconies will be a major bonus for residents. Basement, ground- and first-floor spaces are earmarked for retail/restaurant use, providing improved amenities for Tate visitors and opening the way to a reconfiguration of the public space around the Tate's entrance ramp.

Here is another example of the way in which (relatively, in this case) tall buildings can enhance the London skyline, add new intensity and drama to familiar locales and enhance the public domain.

NORTH ELEVATION

SOUTH ELEVATION

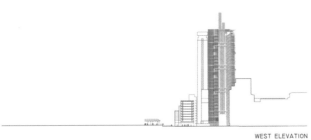

WEST ELEVATION

EAST ELEVATION

Left and opposite
The proposed residential tower at Hopton Street is slightly taller than the chimney of Tate Modern but its slender form minimizes its impact on riverside views and adjacent housing

LOTS ROAD POWER STATION, SW10
TERRY FARRELL & PARTNERS, 2000–06

Sir Terry Farrell (as he became in the summer of 2001) was a pioneer in the cause of adaptive reuse: his phased rehabilitation of the Comyn Ching Triangle in Covent Garden (1978–85) provided a model for similar exercises (now commonplace) across London. Farrell's Lots Road project sees him returning to a mix of conversions and new buildings to revitalize a slice of urban fabric, albeit on a far larger scale.

The power station is a landmark on the Thames, especially memorable on a fine winter day as plumes of smoke drift slowly from its twin 84-metre-high chimneys over Chelsea Reach. It was opened in 1904 as a power source for the Underground, but part of the (widely condemned) privatization programme for the system is making it redundant by obtaining power from other sources, a move that future travellers may have good reason to regret. Farrell's scheme ensures the survival of the building, if not its function.

On Lots Road the steel-framed power station (137 metres long and 43 metres from pavement to the ridge of the roof) is a colossal and overbearing presence: in its day, it was seen as a gross intrusion into the romantic riverside scene. A new building on this scale would be unlikely to gain planning permission. Farrell proposes

to provide nearly 37,000 square metres of residential space within its brick walls, a mix of up-market and social housing, together with shops and restaurants. The 55-metre depth of the power station creates major problems for any conversion. It is proposed to reconstruct the building as two linear apartment blocks, of twelve storeys (on Lots Road) and eight storeys (facing the river), divided by a full-height glazed galleria, a centre for social activity overlooked by the double-aspect apartments. By opening up blocked windows and reglazing the entire building, the power station will acquire a new transparency. On the upper levels, two-storey penthouses will have exceptional river views. The conversion scheme is part of a wider project for integrating the building into its urban context, with new public spaces and routes through the site. There is a price to be paid in terms of achieving commercial viability: a further 33,500 square metres of residential space is proposed in new towers on the river. There are, however, precedents in the area: Eric Lyons's skilfully composed World's End housing and, less happily, the preposterous tower of Chelsea Harbour. The project does not seem likely to meet major planning objections.

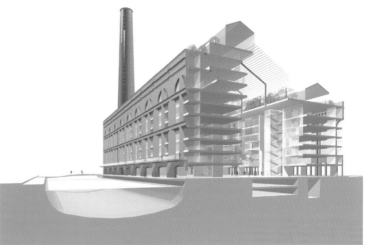

Opposite
Farrell's Lots Road project includes several new residential towers as well as the conversion of the existing power station

Above and right
The power station is to be converted to residential, retail and restaurant use, with the centre of the building occupied by a full-height glazed galleria

MILLENNIUM VILLAGE HOUSING
GREENWICH, SE10

PROCTOR MATTHEWS ARCHITECTS, 1999–2001

Media preoccupation with the fate of the Millennium Dome has deflected attention from the wider context of regeneration plans for the Greenwich Peninsula, until recently a heavily polluted and uninhabited backwater, but now opened up by new public transport facilities. Proctor Matthews' development of 189 residential units, the first of which were occupied at the end of 2000, forms one phase of a 1400-unit village masterplanned by Ralph Erskine near Edward Cullinan's school and health centre.

Described by the architects as "townscape driven", Proctor Matthews' housing responds wholeheartedly to the social commitment of Erskine's plan. It includes both apartment blocks of four to eight storeys and two- and three-storey houses. A group of terraced houses was the first part of the scheme to be completed and occupied, constituting a powerful manifesto for the entire regeneration project. Crisply detailed and colourful – and not over-folksy – the houses

provide an antidote to the drab surroundings: it will be some years before the Millennium Village becomes a self-sufficient community and the first residents must see themselves as pioneers in a great enterprise. The aesthetic has an overall industrial and metallic feel, which is in tune with the extensive use of prefabricated components. This is tempered, however, by the use of vivid colour and natural materials. But it is the interiors of these houses that demonstrate most clearly a determination to erode the barriers between social housing and that produced by the commercial market. This is a socially mixed community, where young professionals will live alongside families from the local authority housing list: full-height windows, flexible plans, double-height spaces and third storeys on some of the houses are features not found in the low-cost housing of the recent past. Landscaping by Robert Rummey will complement the exceptional quality of this development, a leader among a developing London housing scene.

Right and opposite
With their flexible plans, double-height spaces, use of prefabricated components and strong colour, the houses at the Millennium Village provide a striking contrast to those typically offered by developers

Opposite
The Murray Grove housing was constructed to a
tight schedule using prefabricated components

Below
The five-storey building, with apartments accessed
by external galleries, has a scale and urban
character appropriate to its setting

PEABODY HOUSING, MURRAY GROVE, N1

CARTWRIGHT PICKARD ARCHITECTS, 1998–99

Under the leadership of its development director Dickon Robinson, the Peabody Trust (established in 1862 and owner of 20,000 rented homes in London) has emerged as a highly innovative patron of new architecture, seeking to address the continuing shortage of affordable housing and the constantly changing lifestyles of Londoners that have created a demand for something more than the typical 'family home'. Bill Dunster, CZWG and Allford Hall Monaghan Morris are among the practices commissioned by Peabody in the last few years. Robinson is a strong advocate of

increased density: Peabody is currently promoting the construction of a number of residential towers in London.

The housing at Murray Grove, completed in 1999, has a special interest in that the L-shaped, five-storey, thirty-apartment building, on the corner of Murray Grove and Shepherdess Walk, was constructed in only twenty-seven weeks (February–August 1999) using prefabricated modules. The development is arranged in two wings overlooking a landscaped courtyard.

The construction system is as straightforward as a set of toy bricks:

the modules, with plumbing, electrics, doors and windows already attached, are put together to form one-bed (two-module) and two-bed (three-module) units. Access is *via* external galleries along the street frontages, with bathrooms and kitchens placed here to baffle the street noise. On the garden side, overlooked by living and sleeping spaces, each flat has a balcony, large enough to accommodate a dining table: the "industrious artisans" whom Peabody originally set out to house have become sophisticated, though relatively impecunious nurses, teachers and the like.

Murray Grove continues to attract interest as an example of quality housing procured to a fast-track schedule (though the turn-out cost was eventually some 15% more than had been targeted). It is also a very decent piece of urban architecture, well related to the street, with terracotta facing used to reflect the red-brick aesthetic of nearby warehouses, and a strongly expressed lift/staircase tower marking the corner in typically London fashion. As starter homes for young 'key workers', the apartments here set a new standard.

PRIORY HEIGHTS, PRIORY GREEN ESTATE, N1

AVANTI ARCHITECTS, 1998–2000

At first glance, Priory Heights (formerly Wynford House) looks much like hundreds of other local authority housing blocks in London. Closer study of form and details reveals, however, the touch of a master, in this case Berthold Lubetkin, a Modern Movement pioneer whose impact on London was enormous. In the post-war years Lubetkin built on the social promise of the Finsbury Health Centre and moved boldly into the field of housing. The Priory Green Estate was begun in 1948, though Wynford House was not started until 1954, as part of a second phase of development, and completed only in 1957, long after the dissolution of Tecton. It was always intended as a one-off block, though some of the design refinements proposed (internal access by lifts, for example, and private balconies) were omitted on grounds of cost. As usual, it was a matter of false economy, contributing to the downgrading of the estate in more recent years, when extensive demolition was seriously contemplated.

Avanti's refurbishment of Priory Heights has emerged as the marker for an ongoing improvement programme for the entire estate. The block was sold by Islington Council to Community Housing Association in 1997, with Avanti – led by Lubetkin's biographer, John Allan – in charge of the reconstruction project. The block has been reconfigured on the basis of mixed tenure to provide sixty-two private rented units and twenty-six social housing units; this formula generated sufficient revenue to finance a high-quality scheme. Ailing concrete has been restored where necessary, without recourse to crude overcladding, and original finishes and colours have been reinstated. The services, including the lift system, have been comprehensively upgraded. Modern standards of energy efficiency demanded the replacement of the original metal windows, though their substitutes look identical. On top of the building, plant and water-tank installations have been converted into stunning penthouses, with views across London. The project was completed in spring 2000, and all the units were quickly let. Hugely stylish, the project demonstrates one way ahead for London's sometimes problematic stock of post-1945 social housing.

Opposite and left
The Priory Heights project symbolizes huge potential for refurbishing and recycling allegedly obsolete public housing and has spearheaded a regeneration campaign for the estate in which the block stands

10–22 SHEPHERDESS WALK, N1

BUSCHOW HENLEY, 1997–99

A landmark development on the modish border of Shoreditch and Hackney, epicentre of the London art and design world at the beginning of the twenty-first century, Buschow Henley's conversion of a former warehouse in Shepherdess Walk gives definition to the somewhat nebulous concept of the 'loft'.

The raw material was good: a solidly constructed 10,200-square-metre building in two main blocks of five and six storeys around a long central yard. It was opportune, perhaps, that the budget was quite tight. According to the architects, the aims of the project were "pragmatic, reconfiguring the plan, restructuring the building, a series of interconnecting decisions were to subvert the usual order ...

there was not to be an idealized conception".

A particular feature of the building was its division by load-bearing walls into a series of vertical 'tenements', each with its own entrance from the street.

The aim was a mixed-use development: the ground floor is allocated for commercial use, with fifty dual-aspect apartments upstairs. The decision to retain the structural form of the building produced apartments of an L shape – not inconvenient, since it generated an alternative to the conventional (and intrusive) free-standing service core.

The verve with which this project was driven forward by developer and architect is reflected in the treatment of the courtyard

as a generous communal space (the new lift tower is the most prominent addition) and even more in the extraordinary roofscape. With the original proposal of an additional, glazed top floor rejected by planners, a new rooftop scene of detached pavilions, clad in zinc (like the typical Hoxton bar-top) was created. Some of the pavilions have gardens attached – this is "suburbia on the roof". The ad hoc, cumulative approach is in a London, not to say Cockney, tradition: one thinks of the typical East End allotment. Buschow Henley captured the essence of loft living at Shepherdess Walk, with a building that carries the potential for further change and adaptation. This is practical conservation at its best.

Below, left and middle
The project recycled a former warehouse in Shoreditch as a mixed-use development in which the flat roof of the building was colonized with new pavilions and gardens

Below, right, and opposite
The focus of the scheme is the central courtyard, a communal space overlooked by access galleries and punctuated by the new glazed lift tower

THE SKYHOUSE

MARKS BARFIELD ARCHITECTS, 2001–

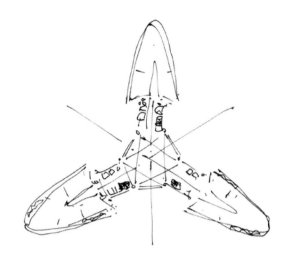

High-rise housing has been widely depicted as the greatest curse to hit London since the Plague: the Ronan Point disaster led to a blanket condemnation of tall blocks of flats. In Britain, they are associated with an under-class; the residents are regarded as victims or prisoners.

David Marks and Julia Barfield's SkyHouse project attacks the presumptions of the recent past head-on: the tall apartment block becomes, not a ghetto, but the setting for the mixed community of the future. Marks Barfield gave London the Eye, the greatest popular success of the millennium. They conceived the idea, developed it into a practical proposition with engineer Jane Wernick, won financial backing for a contentious proposition, and built the 500-foot wheel. The SkyHouse looks equally a winner.

The proposition is to develop a series of towers, up to forty storeys high, arranged in banks of accommodation around communal gardens, with social facilities and shopping, perhaps, provided at lower levels. The petal-like plan is designed to allow natural light to permeate the living quarters and to facilitate a low-energy services strategy.

Marks Barfield has produced a prototype, but it already has its sights on a possible location where a dozen such towers could be constructed: the Greenwich Peninsula, close to the Millennium Dome. The towers would be set in a new park – the size of Battersea Park – with spectacular views over the river to the Thames Estuary in one direction, and to the City and Westminster in the other. Public transport facilities (Alsop's North Greenwich Jubilee line station with the attached interchange by Foster) are excellent. There can be no possible 'heritage' objection to tall buildings here. In short, with the land in public ownership, why don't we get on and build it?

Above and opposite
The SkyHouse, with its winter gardens and controlled use of natural light, is intended as a model for the socially mixed, environmentally responsible, high-density urban communities of the future

STRAW HOUSE AND QUILTED OFFICE
STOCK ORCHARD STREET, N7
SARAH WIGGLESWORTH ARCHITECTS/JEREMY TILL,
1999–2001

Standing hard up against the main railway line into King's Cross, Wigglesworth and Till's Straw House is probably the most-discussed London private house since Future Systems' all-glass Hauer/King House of 1994. The architects wanted a house for their own occupation, plus a professional studio office. The project was seen as a clear demonstration of the principles of sustainability and low-energy design, a potential exemplar for the housing market more generally, rather than an eccentric excursion into the merely avant-garde. At the same time, it has created a beguilingly quiet oasis in the inner-city, a surprisingly calm place for living and working.

Anyone expecting a thatched cottage look is in for a surprise. Straw (barley, it is reported) is used, not in a traditional way, but as a cheap and effective means of insulation, stacked in the form of bales, to cocoon the bedroom wing of the house; inside, they are lime plastered. The main living level is raised above the ground, a place of light and flexible space, illuminated by a wall of protective glazing that filters the sunlight and reduces solar gain. The roof is covered in earth and planted with grass and wild flowers, with a five-floor book tower rising through it and providing a look-out reading room at the top. The office wing extends along the railway, with trains passing every few minutes, so that good acoustic insulation is vital and is provided by a thick layer of sand-filled sacks, raised up on gabions – metal cages filled with crushed waste concrete.

The sustainable credentials of the project are serious: even the book tower has an environmental function, acting as a thermal flue and ventilating the house. Rainwater is collected and used for watering and to supply lavatories and washing machines. The architects claim that their composting toilet is "one of the first to be used in the UK in an urban situation". But there is nothing hair-shirt about the house and studio: its ethos of delight in materials, combined with a sound moral end, seems, indeed, to recall the best aspects of the Arts and Crafts movement, redrawn in the light of twenty-first century issues.

Opposite and left
This live–work settlement in the inner city is a demonstration project in which the potential of sustainable design and low-energy materials is explored

OFFICES

110 BISHOPSGATE
KOHN PEDERSEN FOX

BROADWICK HOUSE, BROADWICK STREET
RICHARD ROGERS PARTNERSHIP

CHISWICK PARK
RICHARD ROGERS PARTNERSHIP

FORMER *DAILY EXPRESS* BUILDING
HURLEY ROBERTSON & ASSOCIATES

J.C. DECAUX HEADQUARTERS
FOSTER & PARTNERS

GREATER LONDON AUTHORITY BUILDING
FOSTER & PARTNERS

HOME OFFICE AND HM PRISON SERVICE HEADQUARTERS
TERRY FARRELL & PARTNERS

LLOYD'S REGISTER OF SHIPPING
RICHARD ROGERS PARTNERSHIP

LONDON BRIDGE TOWER
RENZO PIANO BUILDING WORKSHOP/BROADWAY MALYAN

PADDINGTON BASIN
TERRY FARRELL & PARTNERS/RICHARD ROGERS PARTNERSHIP

PATERNOSTER SQUARE
WHITFIELD PARTNERS (MASTERPLAN)/ALLIES & MORRISON/
MacCORMAC JAMIESON PRICHARD/ERIC PARRY ARCHITECTS/SHEPPARD ROBSON

PORTCULLIS HOUSE (NEW PARLIAMENTARY BUILDING)
MICHAEL HOPKINS & PARTNERS

60 QUEEN VICTORIA STREET
FOGGO ASSOCIATES

SOUTHPOINT, BLACKFRIARS ROAD
ALSOP ARCHITECTS

SWISS RE HEADQUARTERS
FOSTER & PARTNERS

TALKBACK HEADQUARTERS, NEWMAN STREET
BUSCHOW HENLEY

WINCHESTER HOUSE, LONDON WALL
SWANKE HAYDEN CONNELL

88 WOOD STREET
RICHARD ROGERS PARTNERSHIP

110 BISHOPSGATE, EC2

KOHN PEDERSEN FOX, 2000–

110 Bishopsgate – nicknamed Heron Tower after its developer – might appear a relatively uncontroversial project after Norman Foster's Swiss Re sailed through the planning process with backing from the City, English Heritage and the government. In spring 2001, however, a call-in order by Environment Secretary John Prescott stopped the scheme in its tracks and threw its future into question.

This is the second City project by Kohn Pedersen Fox, a practice originating in the United States but rapidly gaining serious credentials in Europe (Thames Court, Upper Thames Street, was finished in 1998). Another major office development by the practice has recently been completed just outside the City on High Holborn. Comparable in scale to Swiss Re and markedly less high than the 1970s Tower 42 (NatWest Tower), Kohn Pedersen Fox's building replaces a group of utterly banal 1970s buildings at Houndsditch, on the eastern boundary of the City. Far removed from the St Paul's Heights control zone, it would form part of a cluster of towers in this part of London, close to excellent public transport facilities. At street level the

scheme would produce real public benefits with part of Houndsditch closed to traffic and turned into a new square, framing the church of St Botolph. The lower levels of the building will be given over to shopping and restaurants, a public domain in marked contrast to the typically private City office lobby. There will be a public restaurant on top of the tower, a response to Mayor Ken Livingstone's call for high buildings to be accessible to all.

The aim has been to produce a highly transparent structure, light and elegant in form, and to instil seriously green ideas into the high building form. The south side of the tower, which faces a busy road, houses a concentration of services that baffle solar gain. On the north side, the building opens up to reveal the stacked three-storey atriums that serve a series of office 'villages'. The east and west façades are designed to provide natural ventilation for the office floors. Intended for multiple occupation by international businesses, the tower addresses the needs of the City as an international financial centre – and it would be a handsome addition to the skyline.

Right and opposite
Though smaller in scale than some recent or proposed additions to the London skyline, Kohn Pedersen Fox's Bishopsgate tower reflects a serious environmental and urban agenda, with façades designed to capitalize on natural light and ventilation, internal gardens and public amenities, including a new square and rooftop restaurant

BROADWICK HOUSE
BROADWICK STREET, W1

RICHARD ROGERS PARTNERSHIP, 1996–2001

In contrast to other current Rogers projects, including Terminal 5, Heathrow, Chiswick Park and the office buildings at Paddington Basin, Broadwick House is, at 4000 square metres and a cost of under £7,000,000, small beer. However, the project underlines the fact that contextual architecture need not be faint-hearted stuff. The site is in the heart of Soho, at the corner of Broadwick Street and Berwick Street (where one of London's liveliest street markets takes place) and is an island, surrounded by streets and lanes. The new six-storey building, let to Ford Motor Company's design division, replaces an undistinguished post-war block. It is an exercise in good manners, though conducted within the framework of a bold approach to design.

The challenge in the scheme was to maximize accommodation on the footprint, while producing a building that is a good neighbour, at home in its surroundings. At street level, a generous set-back on the façades provides precious space for pedestrians on the narrow and often crowded street. Ground floor and basement levels have been let to a restaurant, in tune with the existing character of Soho. The offices are entered *via* a triple aspect reception area on Broadwick Street, spanning the full width of the building. The most distinctive feature of the scheme is the stepping back of the offices at fifth and sixth floors beneath a great arched roof: the double-height top-floor offices have terrific views across the West End, with external terraces as extensions of the working spaces. Offices have floor-to-ceiling glazing, with screening to baffle the sun. A final touch of Rogers style is provided by the panoramic glazed lift tower, which focuses attention on the corner of the building and gives it a dynamic vertical thrust. The use of colour here and in the roof structure relieves an otherwise sombre palette of concrete, aluminium and stainless steel.

Right and opposite
Richard Rogers's Broadwick House is an example of uncompromising and expressive modern design in a historic context, with a finely detailed glazed lift tower forming a powerful marker on the corner of the building and injecting a new dynamism into the Soho street scene

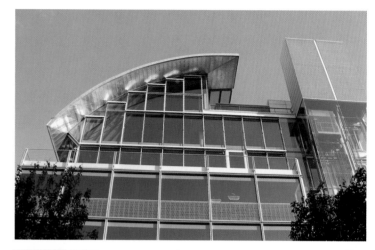

CHISWICK PARK, CHISWICK HIGH ROAD, W4
RICHARD ROGERS PARTNERSHIP, 1999–2003

Left and below
The completed buildings at Chiswick Park – eleven blocks are planned, set in a lush landscape – combine elegant form and careful detailing with speed and economy of construction and a progressive energy strategy to make this the model business park of the twenty-first century

Chiswick Park is one of a number of major London developments thrown into limbo by the 1990s recession and subsequently resurrected. The original masterplan was prepared for Stanhope developers by Terry Farrell. The thirty-three-acre site (formerly a London Transport depot) was cleared and some of the infrastructure carried out. Work then stopped. The present project consists of eleven buildings, all designed by Richard Rogers, with up to 140,500 square metres of space and a working population of ten

thousand. The phased construction process began in 1999.

Stuart Lipton of Stanhope, still an amazingly innovative figure on the London development scene (and a longstanding Rogers client), created the key business park of the 1980s at Stockley Park, near Heathrow. Chiswick Park is emerging as something rather different. First, the diverse architecture of Stockley (Skidmore, Owings & Merrill, Arup, Foster, Eric Parry and others) has given way to an overall look that benefits from the advantages of standardization. Secondly, although there are parking spaces for 1700 cars, most people working at Chiswick will travel there by public transport, using two nearby Underground stations. The new landscape design by W8 provides for a greener and more informal setting than that envisaged by Farrell, with a sizeable park at the core of the development. By placing parking in the undercrofts of the buildings, Rogers avoids the typical business-park look of isolated blocks surrounded by lawns and cars.

The Rogers team has produced a winning formula that combines elegance, economy and adaptability, with the concrete-framed buildings constructed to shell and core stage on a fast-track programme ready for customizing by tenants. The façades incorporate extensive sun screening as part of a low-energy services agenda. Steel columns spaced 6–9 metres away from the blocks support louvre screens, walkways and escape stairs. The rigour of the concept and the quality of the details set this scheme apart, underlining the fact that quality architecture can be achieved on a strict commercial budget, a lesson that Lipton has been preaching for two decades.

FORMER *DAILY EXPRESS* BUILDING
FLEET STREET, EC4

HURLEY ROBERTSON & ASSOCIATES, 1994–2001

The flight of the newspaper industry in the 1980s from Fleet Street to the City fringes and Docklands was prompted by a determination to break traditional union domination and embrace new electronic technology. The large sites that had housed both editorial and printing operations were rapidly redeveloped with deep-span financial services buildings: Kohn Pedersen Fox's reconstruction of the former *Telegraph* complex, incorporating a retained 1930s street frontage, was a typical example of this process.

In 1989 *The Daily Express* was virtually the last of the big papers to quit 'the street

of shame' and the office development planned for its site, extending northwards along Shoe Lane from Fleet Street, subsequently fell victim to the 1990s recession. Owen Williams's remarkable, listed *Express* building – trumpeted, on its opening in 1931, as "Britain's most modern building for Britain's most modern newspaper" – was retained when the remainder of the site was cleared but stood empty and increasingly derelict until Hurley Robertson's 160,000-square-metre office scheme started on site early in 1998, and a major investment bank moved in during spring 2001. As part of this scheme,

Williams's building was painstakingly restored and upgraded – the steel-and-glass cladding, for example, (not strictly a curtain wall) was replicated in line with present-day standards of acoustic and thermal performance. The demolition of a crude 1970s extension on Fleet Street provided an opportunity to create a new curved return elevation on the south-east corner, a stylish reinvention of the Williams manner.

The best-known feature of the *Express* building, its striking Art Deco entrance hall, was the work not of Williams but of Robert Atkinson and incorporated imagery

symbolic of *Express* proprietor Lord Beaverbrook's devotion to the British Empire. Existing elements were carefully conserved and repaired and those that had gone missing – including the extraordinary metal snakes flanking the staircase (stolen at some point in the 1990s) – were replicated. Full-blooded Deco is rare in Britain, and this is one of the best examples to survive. Its restoration is a considerable achievement, and the big new block that has made this rescue operation possible is a decent example of the contemporary commercial style.

Left and opposite
The restoration of the former *Daily Express* building, a 1930s classic, as part of a major office development involved its reinstatement as a distinctive presence on Fleet Street (with later accretions removed) and the restoration of outstanding Art Deco interiors, most notably the entrance hall designed by Robert Atkinson for Lord Beaverbrook

J.C. DECAUX HEADQUARTERS
GREAT WEST ROAD, BRENTFORD
FOSTER & PARTNERS, 1997–2000

Opposite, above
A new glazed 'street', used to display the
company's products, separates the restored 1930s
office wing from the new warehouse building
designed by Foster & Partners for J.C. Decaux

Opposite, below
The 1936 frontage to Great West Road has been
immaculately restored as a setpiece of inter-war
industrial architecture

Below
The new warehouse is an innovative structure,
designed for fast construction and flexible use

Nikolaus Pevsner's famous dismissal of
Wallis Gilbert's Hoover factory of 1932–38
– "perhaps the most offensive of the
modernistic atrocities along this road of
typical by-pass factories" – reflected a
typically Modern Movement attitude to an
architecture of show and, to Pevsner's
mind, deceit. The Grade II listed former
Curry factory, built in 1936, was another
"by-pass factory" of the period, consisting
of a flashy, symmetrical office building,
broadly Deco in style, fronting the road,
with a relatively utilitarian manufacturing
shed hidden away behind. The typical

strategy in revamping buildings of this kind
is to demolish the shed and replace it with
another shed. At the Hoover factory itself,
the famous office frontage is now the
preface to a supermarket, with a smattering
of Deco details to make the new
development fit in.

Working for street furniture manufacturer
J.C. Decaux, Foster was able to apply a
more sophisticated approach. Foster has
designed bus shelters, billboards and other
items for the company, which has a serious
commitment to good modern design. The
office building has been restored in accord

with English Heritage requirements, a
showpiece of 1930s architecture. The new
warehouse behind is a highly innovative
structure, built of pre-cast, thermally
insulated concrete panels allowing fast-
track construction. The interior is lit by a
series of circular roof lights in the
aluminium-clad roof, with the light fittings
integrated into the assembly. The aim is
to secure a warm and even glow inside the
building in all conditions. Warehouse and
offices are separated by a glazed 'street',
which is used to display the company's
products.

GREATER LONDON AUTHORITY BUILDING
LONDON BRIDGE CITY, SE1

FOSTER & PARTNERS, 1998–2002

The new headquarters for the Mayor of London and the GLA was commissioned, controversially, well in advance of the elections held in 2000 that restored to London a measure of strategic local government. In 1998 competing proposals were put forward to house the GLA in Royal Victoria House, Bloomsbury, where a conversion by Will Alsop was on offer, and in a custom-made building developed as part of London Bridge City phase II. The latter option was selected by the government.

After a Classical Revival ('Venice on Thames') scheme designed by John Simpson was abandoned, a new masterplan for the second phase of London Bridge City was commissioned from Foster & Partners. The GLA building can therefore be seen as a spin-off from a commercial development, located in an office ghetto removed from the 'real' London. Yet Foster's building, unkindly caricatured as a "glass testicle" or "fencing mask", is a carefully considered and highly symbolic structure that draws on his experience with the Berlin Reichstag. In total it provides 17,000 square metres of space on ten levels, with offices for mayor, GLA members and their staff, plus committee rooms and public space.

At the heart of the building, however, is the assembly chamber, enclosed in glass, with views across the Thames to the Tower of London. The symbolism is clear: this is a centre of transparent, democratic government, where the electors can watch their representatives at work. The public is welcome in this building (unlike the Palace of Westminster, where its presence is barely tolerated). A top-floor public space will be used for meetings, exhibitions and parties, and above that is a public rooftop terrace. The building is surrounded by a public piazza. Internal circulation *via* lifts and ramps provides access for all.

The form of the building has symbolic undertones but is also a reflection of a determined effort to secure optimum energy performance. Cladding has been designed to respond to patterns of sunlight falling on the building. Active and passive shading devices are part of a programme of natural ventilation, with cooling provided using ground water pumped from boreholes below the building, which looks set to become an instantly recognizable London landmark. Mayor Ken Livingstone was initially critical of the project, but the building could indirectly strengthen his campaign for extending local democracy in the capital.

Opposite
The assembly chamber at the heart of the GLA
building is a transparent and open space, with
views out to the river and City, that echoes
Norman Foster's Berlin Reichstag project

Right and below
The glazed form of the building is dynamic, even
forceful, with a sophisticated cladding system
designed to control solar gain and provide
benign working conditions

HOME OFFICE AND HM PRISON SERVICE HEADQUARTERS, MARSHAM STREET, SW1

TERRY FARRELL & PARTNERS, 1998–2004

The group of three 1960s government office slabs at Marsham Street, long occupied by the Department of the Environment, has generally been condemned as a monstrous intrusion into the London skyline. In fact, the complex (designed by the Property Services Agency under Eric Bedford) has a stark power of its own, though it forms an unfortunate backcloth to the towers of Westminster in views from the river. After years of apparent indecision, however, and the abandonment of at least one redevelopment project, the Marsham Street towers appear to be heading for demolition.

Terry Farrell's masterplan, originating in the planning consent given for the redevelopment of the site in 1997, seeks to achieve high density, with accommodation for three thousand civil servants, combined with urbanity and the restoration of what Farrell sees as an appropriate scale – "a new and vibrant civic community with a strong sense of place". Three medium-rise blocks (up to seven storeys) are proposed, forming a symmetrical group of central pavilion and wings. Each is focused around a full-height glazed atrium. By stepping the blocks, Farrell seeks to link the development to its mostly low-rise context.

For Farrell, response to urban grain and character matters more than extravagant architectural gestures. He aims to reintegrate the site into the city. As yet, the details of the project remain necessarily sketchy, while the prospect that it will be procured by the Private Funding Initiative might sound alarm bells on its eventual quality. The development should surely rise above typical spec-office quality – a hint of its aspirations is found in Farrell's proposed entrance block, with its strongly expressed stone portico and full-height, five-storey glazed screen reflecting the public nature of the scheme. That, at least, is the theory; one hopes that it survives into the completed buildings.

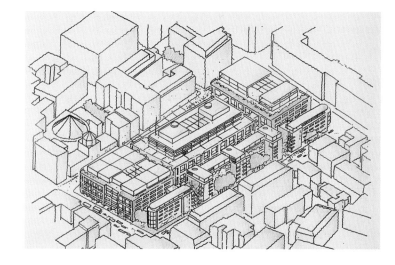

Above
Farrell's masterplan for Marsham Street replaces the existing 1960s office slabs with a dense new urban quarter in which social and public spaces punctuate large office floorplates

Opposite
Lofty glazed atriums, enclosing dense planting, provide a focus for the new office buildings, which have a formal dignity in tune with their status

LLOYD'S REGISTER OF SHIPPING FENCHURCH STREET, EC3

RICHARD ROGERS PARTNERSHIP, 1995–2000

Back in 1993 Richard Rogers had been commissioned to prepare a scheme to move Lloyd's Register, a venerable City institution, from Fenchurch Street to a green-belt site at Liphook, Hampshire. The organization saw little prospect of redeveloping in the conservation area around its splendid 1900s headquarters, but the proposed move to Hampshire foundered on planning objections. By 1995 Lloyd's Register had resolved to remain in the City and Rogers prepared a scheme that combined new construction with refurbishment. On Lloyd's Avenue, all existing façades had to be retained and the listed headquarters building was to be meticulously restored.

The site could not have been more problematic, with listed buildings and the remains of an ancient churchyard to cope with. Its confined nature made it difficult to ensure adequate amounts of natural light, though there were advantages in developing the new building within a protective shell of retained structures. An oasis of tranquil space, a quiet and relatively unpolluted refuge from the City streets, could be created, with the new building extending skywards within it to secure daylight and views.

As completed (and occupied since 2000), Lloyd's Register consists of two glazed slabs of accommodation, twelve and fourteen storeys tall, connected to six storeys of additional space behind retained façades on Lloyd's Avenue. The three

buildings, arranged on a fan-shaped grid (which produced slightly tapered floorplates), are connected by glazed atriums. The former churchyard, long buried and forgotten within the City block, has re-emerged as an attractive public space, with the landscape extending into the internal atriums. The contrast between this ancient space and the transparent service towers, with fully glazed wall-climber lifts constantly in motion, reflect the dynamism of the twenty-first-century City. This is a finely crafted building, assembled of pre-cast concrete, with carefully detailed 'servant' cores for circulation and services made of brightly coloured steel.

The concrete structure of the building, left exposed in the office ceilings, with their chilled beams, is part of a strategy for low-energy running that also includes the use of extensive shading devices that give the east and west façades a strongly modelled character.

The balance of new design and conservation in this project is a response to the particular circumstances of the City; nobody doubted the importance of the original headquarters, for example. But the omission of Rogers's entrance pavilion on Fenchurch Street, an elegant structure, modestly slotted between Collcutt's 1901 building and a handsome listed pub, in favour of the retention of an unlisted building of no special interest was an example of the balance being lost.

Opposite
Rogers's Lloyd's Register develops the language of 'served and servant' spaces seen in his earlier City masterpiece, Lloyd's of London, using a high degree of glazing to channel natural light into the confined site

Above
Lofty glazed atriums separate the office wings and filter controlled daylight into workspaces

LONDON BRIDGE TOWER, SE1

RENZO PIANO BUILDING WORKSHOP/BROADWAY MALYAN,
2000–05

The London Bridge Tower could become, like Norman Foster's Millennium Tower, one of London's great unbuilts. Firmly opposed by English Heritage and other interests, it could remain as nothing more than a vision. Yet one has to take developer Irvine Sellar seriously when he speaks of a "global landmark ... a building of which Londoners can be rightly proud": projects such as this are not the most obvious way to make profits out of property and, like all tower-builders, Sellar seems to be driven by considerations wider than the purely financial.

Initial proposals were drawn up by Broadway Malyan, but towards the end of 2000 the Genoese master Renzo Piano was brought in to rethink the scheme, intended to replace a dreary 1970s office tower adjacent to London Bridge station. At this stage, the new building was to be 390 metres high, easily the tallest habitable building in Europe. By the time of the planning submission in 2001, its height had been cut to 306 metres – not enough of a reduction to satisfy the anti-tower lobby. London mayor Ken Livingstone, however, emerged as a strong supporter of the project, which also won backing from the Commission for Architecture and the Built Environment. With 80,000 square metres of office, hotel and residential space over a main transport hub, the tower is in accord with Livingstone's environmental and regenerative strategies and would be a huge booster to the economy of Southwark.

Piano has compared his designs to "a shard of glass" – he considers the slender, spire-like form of the tower a positive addition to the London skyline and believes that its presence will be far more ethereal than opponents of the scheme allege. Piano's preoccupation with the appropriate use of materials – stone, wood, steel, glass – is famous and has produced a diverse range of buildings. At London Bridge, he proposes a sophisticated use of glazing, with expressive façades of angled panes intended to reflect light and the changing patterns of the sky, so that the perceived form of the building will vary with the weather and the seasons. It will be anchored to the site by a base containing shops, restaurants and exhibition and conference spaces where up to ten thousand people could work.

Oddly, the projections of the tower's impact used as ammunition by its opponents do not make it look overbearing. Rather, it appears as a memorable landmark, far removed from the conventional idea of an office block. It may well be unbuildable, but if it were to be built it would become an instant symbol of London.

Below and opposite
Renzo Piano's London Bridge Tower has been designed as a light and transparent needle, a shapely contrast to the lumpish slabs that surround the site, and sits comfortably in historic Borough

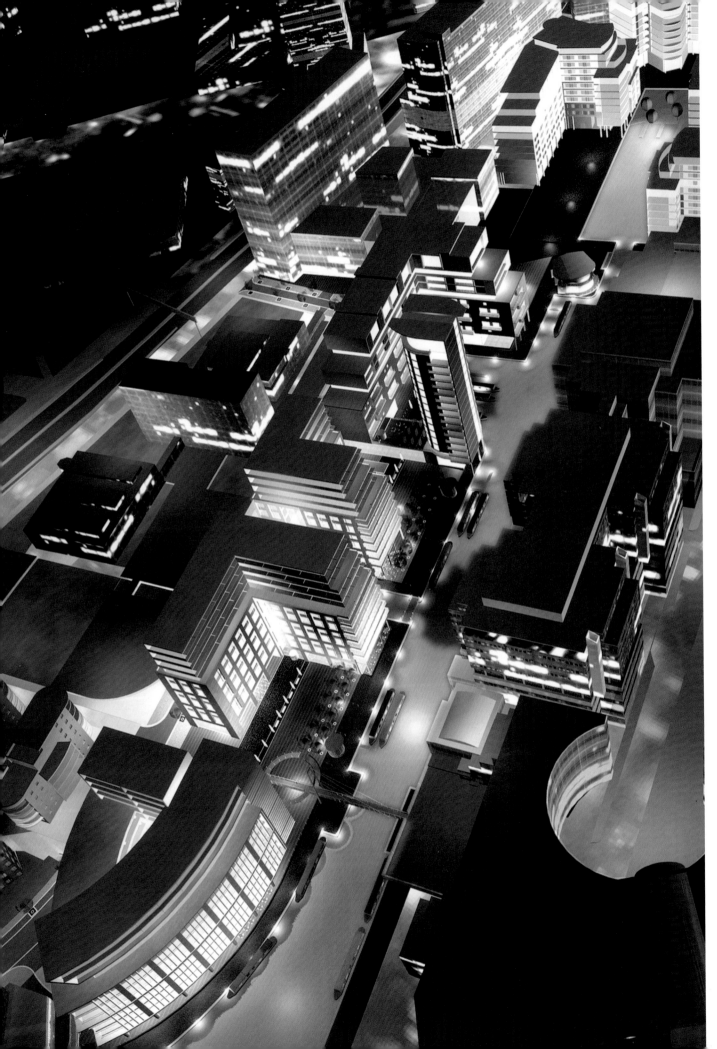

Left
The masterplan for
Paddington Basin
proposes an intensive
commercial and residential
development close to
Paddington station, itself
scheduled for major
reconstruction

Opposite, above
Terry Farrell's The Point is
the first building on the
site to be completed: its
wedge shape responds to
the curve in the Grand
Union Canal at this point

Opposite, below
A high-rise, mixed-use
building by Richard Rogers
Partnership is envisaged
as the focal point of the
development, but may
founder on objections by
Westminster City Council

PADDINGTON BASIN, W2

TERRY FARRELL & PARTNERS/
RICHARD ROGERS PARTNERSHIP, 2000–

The area around Paddington station – a ten-acre site focusing on the basin of the Grand Union Canal, plus the former Great Western Railway goods yard – forms the largest development site in the City of Westminster, potentially a Canary Wharf for central London. The model of Canary Wharf, indeed – lots of offices plus housing for the affluent – seems to have fuelled the ongoing plans for the site, though the area might have been integrated into the city and become a model for mixed-use development.

Paddington has had a long wait for the regeneration bandwagon. A 110,000-square-metre office project for the Basin, plus retailing and residential development, designed by Building Design Partnership and Skidmore, Owings & Merrill, won detailed planning consent in 1992 but fell

victim to the recession. Renewed developer interest in the area has been partly stimulated by transport improvements – the Heathrow Express, the prospect of CrossRail (first planned in the 1980s) actually happening, and the proposed reconstruction and extension of the mainline station, with new links to the goods yard and Basin. The goods yard is now being transformed by Development Securities, with an intensive 175,000-square-metre office and residential scheme masterplanned by Sidell Gibson (previous plans for the site were drawn up by Seifert & Partners).

The Basin development was successfully relaunched by a partnership between Godfrey Bradman of European Land and Property and Chelsfield's Elliott Bernerd. The masterplan was prepared by

Terry Farrell and provides for a more dynamic mix, in terms of scale and forms, than was envisaged in the early 1990s. Phase one, on the north side of the Basin, will contain 140,000 square metres of offices and apartments.

The Point, designed by Farrell, is the first of the buildings to get off the ground. A ten-storey, 20,500-square-metre wedge-shaped office scheme with the sleek styling typical of Farrell's recent work, it forms a gateway to the Basin. Richard Rogers Partnership is responsible for three buildings so far, two of thirteen storeys, plus a mixed-use tower located on the northerly edge of the site, close to the A40. The building actually consists of three connected towers, the tallest of forty storeys, containing offices, hotel, apartments, arts and leisure facilities

and public viewing galleries. It could be the model for a new generation of tall buildings in London, elegant in form, mixed in use and progressive in terms of its servicing and energy strategy. Unfortunately, the tower seems likely to be abandoned in the face of opposition from Westminster Council (which had previously identified Paddington as a suitable location for high buildings) and from English Heritage, with its visibility from Hyde Park a major issue.

The reconstruction of Paddington station by Railtrack will include a major office scheme designed by Nicholas Grimshaw. Plans for a forty-two-storey tower were announced in 2000, with a new public concourse to the canal. The tower, however, has been abandoned in Grimshaw's latest proposals for the station.

PATERNOSTER SQUARE
CITY OF LONDON, EC4

WHITFIELD PARTNERS (MASTERPLAN)/ALLIES & MORRISON/
MacCORMAC JAMIESON PRICHARD/ERIC PARRY
ARCHITECTS/SHEPPARD ROBSON, 1997–

Included here as the distinctly downbeat conclusion to a long-running saga that has involved many of the biggest names in British architecture and a succession of owners/developers, the Paternoster Square development, yards from St Paul's Cathedral, occupies one of the most prominent sites in the whole of London. The location had the potential to generate a new quarter of outstanding quality: it seems unlikely to do so.

The dense area of Victorian offices and warehouses around the old Paternoster Square was levelled by German bombs in 1940. It was rebuilt, in line with a masterplan by Sir William Holford and with Trehearne & Norman as architects, in 1961–67 as a rather bland complex of offices set on a raised service deck around public spaces which, though generous in scale, were always underused. Never much loved, the rebuilt seven-acre quarter seemed an obvious location for the deep-plan office spaces demanded by the post-'Big Bang' City. In 1986 a starry team of practices, including Foster, Rogers, Stirling, Skidmore, Owings & Merrill, Isozaki and MacCormac, was invited to prepare redevelopment proposals. The more radical ideas – such as Foster's 'souk' of interlocking office spaces and pedestrian routes and Rogers's dramatic daylit Underground concourse – found no favour and a classically inclined (though formally Modern) scheme by Arup Associates was selected in 1987. Though subsequently beefed up with contributions from Michael Hopkins and Richard MacCormac, the Arup masterplan was later dropped after strident criticism from the Prince of Wales (whose

influence was then at its zenith). The prince backed alternative, Classical Revival plans by John Simpson, strongly influenced by the urban thinking of Leon Krier. After a change of developers, Simpson was brought in as masterplanner, working – uncomfortably, perhaps – with Terry Farrell (then in Post-modernist mode) and American Thomas Beeby. Individual blocks were designed by Demetri Porphyrios, Quinlan Terry and others. The scheme got planning consent in 1993 and was then quietly abandoned. Sir William Whitfield, a senior figure adept at marrying modernity and tradition and a former Surveyor of St Paul's, was brought in as masterplanner in 1997.

Once the subject of intense, even bitter, debate and extensive media coverage, Paternoster Square has now become just another large office development. Although Michael Hopkins has quit the scene, the practices involved are ones skilled at working imaginatively in historic contexts (look at MacCormac's Oxbridge projects). Yet the dead hand of the masterplan, with its lifeless sub-classical loggia enclosing a tightly hemmed-in piazza, has wrung the life out of their architecture. The completed development will be well-crafted, polite, efficient, a convenient place to do business – but no more. It represents a retreat from the expansive City mood of the new century and its public spaces are unlikely to be as inviting as those of, for example, Broadgate. Paternoster Square is an area that architecture-minded visitors to London would be advised to explore only as an example of the depths to which English 'good taste' has sunk.

Opposite and below
After many years of debate, the redevelopment of
Paternoster Square, close to St Paul's Cathedral,
is under way but the scheme, choreographed by
Sir William Whitfield, looks likely to produce a
series of inoffensive but dull buildings in a weak
compromise between modernity and tradition

PORTCULLIS HOUSE
(NEW PARLIAMENTARY BUILDING)
VICTORIA EMBANKMENT, SW1

MICHAEL HOPKINS & PARTNERS, 1989–2000

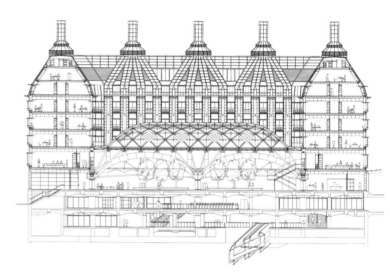

After several decades of indecision – an earlier project for an extension to the Houses of Parliament by Spence & Webster was abandoned – the commission for a new parliamentary building, with office and committee room accommodation for the House of Commons, went to Michael Hopkins & Partners in 1989. In the same year, legislation providing for the construction of the Jubilee line extension, with a new interchange station at Westminster, was tabled. With the existing Underground station located directly underneath the site of what became Portcullis House, the two projects seemed inseparable. In 1991 Hopkins was appointed architect for the new station and construction began early in 1994. After Members of Parliament vetoed the idea of a station concourse below Parliament Square, the new booking hall was to be sited directly beneath the central courtyard of the new parliamentary building, with the District line tracks operating throughout construction work a level below. The structure of Portcullis House is integrated with that of the station, and the two projects, both completed during 2000, ran in parallel. The great columns on which Portcullis House stands extend down 40 metres into the station box, accommodating the diagonal route of the District line and the banks of escalators serving the Jubilee line platforms.

The structural challenge of the project was enormous. Given the cultural and architectural climate of 1980s Britain, however, the aesthetic challenge of designing a contemporary building adjacent to Pugin and Barry's Palace of Westminster, a national icon, was hardly less daunting. The completed building takes its scale from Norman Shaw's neighbouring Scotland Yard (now used by the Commons), which also provides the cue for the massive thermal chimneys. The picturesque if rather industrial chimneys are integral to a low-energy ventilation strategy, also reflected in a plan that disposes naturally lit offices around a central court. At ground-floor level the court forms a social and circulation space for the complex, enclosed by a finely crafted roof of glass, laminated timber and steel – a reinterpretation of the innovative tradition which inspired the great fourteenth-century roof of Westminster Hall, which sits on the six main structural columns. Largely inaccessible to the public, this is one of the most impressive contemporary spaces in London, connected by tunnel to the Palace of Westminster. The exterior of Portcullis House below roof level is more mannered, though its logic is impeccable: vertical stone bands, diminishing in width as they rise, frame window bays formed of bronze. Planned under Thatcher and opened under Blair, Portcullis House is genuinely contextual – and more innovative than some negative critics allow. Built to last a century, it has already become an accepted part of the riverside scene. Will it outlive the institution it houses?

Above
Michael Hopkins's extension to the Palace of Westminster, structurally a unit with the station below, represents a brave attempt at modern contextualism that has produced a forceful, if mannered, addition to the riverside scene

Opposite
The central court of Portcullis House is covered by a glazed roof, constructed of steel and laminated timber, that sits on the main columns that also form the structure of the Underground station

60 QUEEN VICTORIA STREET
BLACKFRIARS, EC4
FOGGO ASSOCIATES, 1990–2000

Queen Victoria Street, a nineteenth-century creation once lined with Victorian commercial palazzi, has been progressively redeveloped since the 1950s, mostly to bleak effect. The most prominent (and contentious) recent development is Stirling Wilford's Number 1 Poultry, designed in the late 1980s but completed after James Stirling's death and replacing a group of Victorian listed buildings. The Foggo building occupies the next site to the west on Queen Victoria Street. While Number 1 Poultry is a one-off, the outcome of thirty years of planning and debate, 60 Queen Victoria Street illustrates a wider trend towards quality in new City buildings.

Peter Foggo (who died in 1993) obtained a planning consent for the site in 1990, soon after his departure from Arup Associates, where he was lead designer for the huge 1980s Broadgate development. The built 15,000-square-metre scheme, however, dates from 1997. The new building efffectively fills the roughly triangular site, with wings of office space along Queen Victoria Street and Queen Street and a glazed atrium facing a narrow side street at the rear.

Building in the City is never easy: the planners demanded gravitas and an element of solidity in the exteriors while the client naturally wanted large, flexible floors with plenty of natural light and a good net-to-gross ratio. The resulting building manages to be honest, in a way that most 1980s Post-modern office buildings are not, efficient and handsome. The planning is masterly, with access *via* a corner lobby – a neat restatement of the traditional Victorian arrangement. What is most distinctive about the building is, however, its façade treatment. Rather than stone, the architects opted for patinated bronze, which provides the building with instant ageing, with *brise-soleil* grilles to baffle the sun on the main elevations. Seven floors of offices are set on a strongly modelled base, with bronze columns and cantilevers supporting the framework of façade grilles.

Opposite
The façades of this new City office building respond to dictates of site and climate, with heavy shading to the south and west and a greater degree of transparency on the sheltered northern elevation

Left
The fastidious detailing of the building introduces a new element of visual interest into the City streets, though the rationale is more functional than decorative

SOUTHPOINT, BLACKFRIARS ROAD, SE1

ALSOP ARCHITECTS, 1999–

The Southpoint project – a 28,000-square-metre landmark office building opposite Richard MacCormac's Southwark station – is a product of the 'Southwark effect', the boom in development south of the river fuelled by the Jubilee line extension and Tate Modern and facilitated by an enterprise-friendly local authority and the dynamic regeneration agenda set by planner Fred Manson. The scheme reflects Will Alsop's steady rise to the centre of the London scene and his clear emergence as a front-rank commercial architect: his designs are no longer seen as fanciful or unbuildable.

The building replaces Orbit House, an unremarkable 1960s block by Seifert that provides a depressing introduction to the borough for millions of Tate Modern visitors using Southwark station. Proximity to the Underground was a strong attraction, while the prospect of Thameslink 2000 operating from nearby Blackfriars, with regular airport links, contributes to its appeal.

The key idea of the scheme is that of a series of horizontal planes, the lowest tilted off the ground to provide a dynamic public space that recognizes the new role of Southwark as a tourist location, with streets full of people. The central office zone of the building forms a 'cloud' floating above Southwark. A proposed top slab, containing executive offices, was later deleted on the recommendation of planners. Southpoint not only looks radical – its polychromatic façades make use of the latest glazing technology, with ceramic inks indelibly bonded into the glass, to break down the rigid geometry of the office floors – but equally represents a fresh look at the large office building. The 30-metre-wide floors are designed for maximum flexibility and are enhanced by double-height spaces, mezzanines and terraces. An intermediate glazed zone between the first and second planes provides a social space for the building's users, a recognition of the primacy of interaction in the new office. At street level, cafés and shops cater for both building users and for the public: the barrier between the office and the public domain is eroded.

Opposite and right
Will Alsop's Southpoint is a landmark
development in the transformation of the
Bankside area – it replaces a banal 1960s
block – and is innovative in form, materials
and in its radical view of the workplace, as
well as its contribution to the public realm

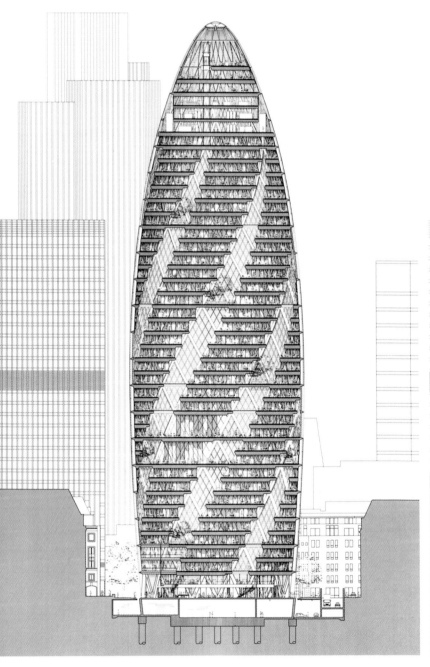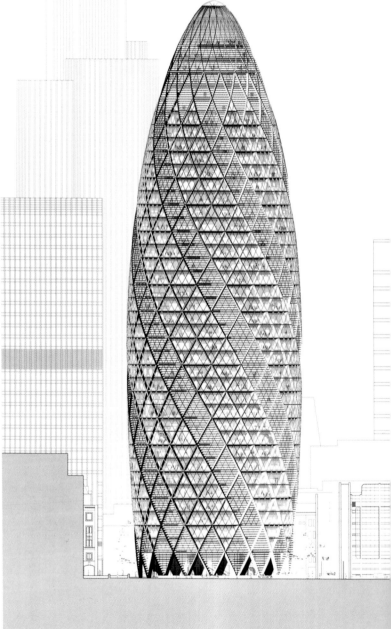

SWISS RE HEADQUARTERS
ST MARY AXE, EC3
FOSTER & PARTNERS, 1997–2004

Swiss Re was one of half a dozen or more City of London office schemes by Foster & Partners on site or planned in 2001. Yet it stands out from the rest in terms not only of its prominence on the skyline – at forty-one storeys, it competes for attention with the slightly taller Tower 42 (formerly NatWest Tower) – but even more for its technical and environmental innovation. Indeed, Swiss Re is one of the key Foster projects of the new century.

The site is that of the Baltic Exchange, a sumptuous but rather dim Edwardian commercial palazzo damaged beyond repair by an IRA bomb in 1992. Foster's first proposal for the site was the London Millennium Tower, a proposal that aroused strong opposition from amenity groups and found little favour with the City Corporation.

With Swiss Re (a major reinsurance company) as client, Foster developed a new scheme for "London's first ecological tall building". The 40,000-square-metre project has its origins in Norman Foster's exploratory work with Buckminster Fuller on the Climatroffice, where green garden spaces would be integrated into the workplace, and develops ideas seen in the seminal 1970s Willis Faber offices and, more recently, in the Frankfurt Commerzbank (with its 'sky gardens'). Foster's partner Ken Shuttleworth has compared Swiss Re to "a series of Willis Fabers, piled vertically, one on top of the other". A developed version of the Commerzbank sky garden is used both as a social focus and as part of a low-energy environmental strategy: stale air will be

drawn into the gardens and re-oxygenated by the dense planting. (Ventilation is largely by natural, non-mechanical means; air conditioning is used only in a supplementary role and windows are made to open.) The office floors spiral around the gardens, forming vertical 'villages' that are intended to generate the interaction increasingly seen as vital to creative office work. Lifts, stairs and other services are concentrated in a central core, leaving the fully-glazed perimeter free of intrusions.

At street level the painstaking aerodynamic modelling of the tower has been calculated to avoid down draughts and ensure benign conditions in the new piazza that surrounds the building. Two floors of the building will be given over to a shopping arcade. A restaurant and bar are

planned for the top of the tower, uncompromised by the usual clutter of plant.

Swiss Re has injected a new element into a continuing debate about the place of high buildings in London. It reinforces the point that office towers can be distinctive, even beautiful, objects that complement, rather than deface, the skyline. It also undermines the contention that tall buildings are environmentally irresponsible, dependent on huge amounts of energy. For all this, it is a prestige commission, a bespoke work for a client whose name and reputation can only benefit from an act of enlightened patronage.

Opposite
The Swiss Re tower is likely to be one of the most remarkable of Norman Foster's buildings of the early twenty-first century and is innovative both structurally and environmentally: a series of internal gardens is a key element of the project

Right
The building will have a distinctive and dramatic presence on the skyline, its shapely form contrasting with the more conventional geometry of earlier high buildings in the City

TALKBACK HEADQUARTERS NEWMAN STREET, W1

BUSCHOW HENLEY, 1999–2001

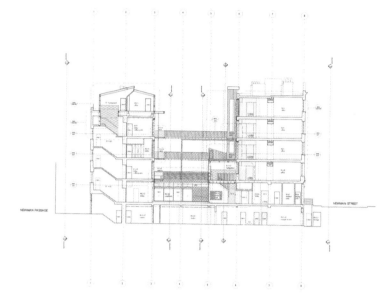

Buschow Henley's mixed-use adaptation at Shepherdess Walk, Hoxton, was an object lesson in how to reuse old industrial buildings, adding new elements without draining them of character and patina. The youthful practice's strong concern for materials and their appropriate use was reflected in the project. The new headquarters for TalkBack TV just north of Oxford Street embraces similar concerns, though both location and the raw material that forms the basis of the project are very different.

TalkBack TV is a production company with a strong creative bent that employs up to two hundred and fifty people. The commissioning of its new London base involved the development not only of a functional brief but also a searching examination of the ethos and aspirations of the company, which sees itself as straddling the worlds of business and research/education. It is concerned with ideas and with individuals, a non-hierarchical organization that is about interaction and communication. In the past, it has inhabited a string of premises across the West End. The informality of this arrangement, but not its inconvenience, is valued.

The new building is an adaptation of two six-storey blocks, sturdily built but of uncertain date (c.1900?) and no special architectural interest, on Newman Street,

separated by a courtyard from a rear five-storey block on to the narrow Newman Passage. The architects' proposal was to form a multi-storey cloister by demolishing a two-storey linking block and inserting a new structure into the gap. This structure houses communal facilities for the complex, with a reception area and meeting and common rooms around an open court. Studio spaces are at basement level, insulated from noise. First-floor roof gardens are part of an effort to create a quiet oasis, apparently removed from the noisy streets beyond. The central space is the focus of the development, with offices served by timber decks that are intended as places of interaction as well as of circulation. The Newman Passage building has been given an additional floor. Timber is used extensively, along with galvanized steel, zinc and aluminium; existing brickwork, in generally good condition, has been left much as found. The lift tower has been made into a landmark 'campanile', clad in Douglas-fir boarding, with a cutaway at the top to expose the works.

This project illustrates the way in which relatively ordinary buildings can be given a unique quality and customized to the needs of state-of-the-art organizations. Buschow Henley's project transforms what existed, but equally responds to the secret world of backyards and rooftops behind the blank Victorian façades.

Above
The TalkBack project colonizes a previously underused area at the core of a West End block, linking two existing buildings with a new block containing the reception area and meeting rooms

Opposite
The additions to the Victorian blocks have been made in a lightweight manner, using a variety of materials, including the Douglas-fir cladding applied to the new lift shaft

WINCHESTER HOUSE, LONDON WALL, EC2

SWANKE HAYDEN CONNELL, 1995–99

The shifting tide of planning and design policies in the City – ranging from determinedly preservationist to ardently *laissez-faire* – poses enormous problems for developers seeking to provide for global financial industries. By 2001 the City was looking favourably on proposals for tall buildings and questioning established conservation strategies. A few years earlier, the discreet ground-scraper was *de rigueur.* Swanke Hayden Connell's Winchester House remains one of the best examples of the genre. (The same practice has more recently completed an even larger building for Merrill Lynch, buried behind retained frontages at Newgate.)

Pevsner described the 1960s Winchester House, demolished for this development, as "reticent and anonymous" – dull and mean would be equally suitable adjectives for this twenty-two-storey tower, which occupied only 25% of the total site area. The redevelopment had to take account (as the 1960s scheme did not) of the group of listed buildings, including the Neo-classical church of All Hallows, that surround the site. The existence of a vast parking basement was a 1960s asset worth retaining: it was used for plant and services, rather than parking, to free the upper levels of the new building.

The new Winchester House fills the site, reinstating the dignity of the narrow Great Winchester Street (previously downgraded to a service road). On this elevation the scheme is broken down into a series of units – town houses – in deference to the scale of the street. On London Wall the use of set-backs reduces the apparent bulk and height of the ten-storey building. Sandstone is used to good effect as a cladding material; during the late 1990s, stone facings were inevitably imposed on all City developments. The leasing of the building to Deutsche Bank, famous as a patron of contemporary art, has made the exceptionally generous reception area into a gallery. How unfortunate that the public can only peer through the glass doors.

Left
The unusually generous reception lobby is used as a gallery for the display of an outstanding collection of contemporary art

Right and opposite
The use of stone cladding and set-backs gives the London Wall elevation a scale and dignity appropriate to its context and represents a bold reversal of the tower/piazza planning of the 1960s, while the rear elevation is articulated to address a minor City street

88 WOOD STREET, EC2
RICHARD ROGERS PARTNERSHIP, 1990–99

88 Wood Street was Richard Rogers's first City building since the completion of Lloyd's of London in 1986. The commission came to the practice in 1990, when the brief was for a prestige headquarters for the Japanese Daiwa corporation. Delays in securing consent to demolish a listed building on the site proved fatal to this project: recession in London and the Far East killed it.

When Daiwa revived the scheme in 1993, it was with the intention of building a straightforward speculative office development. The existing proposals could not be adapted to the changed brief and the project was entirely redesigned in 1993–94 and constructed in 1995–99.

The completed building consists of three linked parallel blocks that step up from eight storeys on Wood Street (where the development faces the Grade I listed Wren tower of St Alban's church and the Neo-classical police station by McMorran & Whitby) to fourteen and finally to eighteen storeys.

88 Wood Street has the strong stamp of the Rogers office. The tower-like service cores, for example, are in the Lloyd's tradition, but plant was banished, as far as possible, to the basement so that the slender towers of the three primary cores contain only toilets and lifts, with highly glazed staircases attached. The lifts sit within a glazed enclosure, so that transparency is combined with protection from the weather. The service towers are steel-framed, while the main structure is of concrete, though the steel bracing reinforces the metallic look of the building. Colour is used boldly, in the Rogers manner, on the staircases and sculptural services extractors at street level.

The context of the scheme is mostly post-war and extraordinarily varied: the Rogers building is sandwiched between unremarkable new office developments by Foster & Partners and Sheppard Robson and slammed up against Terry Farrell's showy 1980s Albangate, with the dramatic towers of the Barbican as a backcloth. It stands out in this setting as something more than a 'good ordinary' City office building. It is the transparency and lightness of 88 Wood Street that is memorable, achieved firstly by skilful massing that allows natural light to permeate the office floors. The use of crystal-clear glass, with floor-to-ceiling panels within the grid, is uncompromising in a way that is typical of Rogers. The entrance lobby has a nobility of scale rarely found in Britain, with internal and external landscape merging to embrace the remains of an ancient churchyard. London needs more commercial architecture of this quality.

Opposite
The entrance lobby at 88 Wood Street is one of the grandest in London, its luminous interior seamlessly linked to the reconfigured external landscape

Above
The building consists of three linked blocks, the lowest facing Wood Street, with services used in typical Rogers fashion to articulate the architecture

SHOPS

CARTIER, OLD BOND STREET
JEAN-MICHEL WILMOTTE

MARNI, SLOANE STREET
FUTURE SYSTEMS

PETER JONES, SLOANE SQUARE
JOHN McASLAN & PARTNERS

SAINSBURY'S, GREENWICH PENINSULA
CHETWOOD ASSOCIATES

CARTIER, 40–41 OLD BOND STREET, W1

JEAN-MICHEL WILMOTTE, 2000

While many fashion retailers aim at spectacular and even bizarre effects in their premises, Cartier has sought a more classic, though essentially contemporary, elegance, combining tradition with modernity, in its series of boutiques designed by French architect Jean-Michel Wilmotte. The first two opened in Paris and Tokyo in 1999.

The façade of the new London shop is made from slate, a matt material that effectively frames the anti-reflection glass of the windows and provides the element of sobriety, tranquillity and restraint that the client desired. Sparkling black Norwegian stone is used for the internal façade, while the floors are laid in light Italian stone. The woodwork is a mixture of grained oak and rosewood, with metallic finishes of velvet nickel. Wilmotte's fit-out draws on his extensive experience of public and museum commissions – for example, the interiors of the Grand Louvre. Furniture was specially designed by Pierre Deltombe (whose previous jobs include the design of the visitor facilities at the Sainte-Chapelle in Paris) while diffused lighting animates the 'jewel box' interior with its series of intimate spaces.

In Britain, 'luxury' usually implies a firmly traditional look that often descends to weak pastiche: London lacks classic modern retail interiors. (Simpson's, Piccadilly, was recently spoiled by conversion to a bookstore.) Wilmotte's work for Cartier has a timeless quality that combines elegance and a suggestion of minimalism with the degree of comfort and reassurance that anyone considering spending £50,000 on an engagement ring might appreciate.

Left and opposite
Cartier's new London shop makes use of high-quality materials – stone, wood, leather and glass – to achieve an effect that is opulent without being showy, in keeping with the company's image

MARNI, SLOANE STREET, SW3

FUTURE SYSTEMS, 2000

Shops come and go: twenty years ago, Norman Foster's wonderfully light and elegant store for Joseph was one of the sights of Sloane Street. Jan Kaplicky and Amanda Levete of Future Systems come out of Foster's high-tech stable, but their work has a sensual, illusionistic, even baroque, quality that Foster eschews. They are, in other words, natural shop designers and the Marni store, one of a projected chain to be developed by this Milan-based company (branches are planned for Milan and Tokyo), is in a tradition of retail design that includes major works in London by David Chipperfield, Branson Coates and others. Selfridge's commission to the practice to design a new store in Birmingham was an extraordinary breakthrough.

The shop makes its mark on the style-conscious street with a frontage forged of stainless steel membrane, a mere 1.3 millimetres thick. Inside, the space is typically long and narrow. The clothes are hung or displayed on rails formed as steel trees cantilevered out of the floor: the merchandise is as much the focus of the place as the art in a gallery.

The backcloth to the interior is strongly coloured, forming a contrast to the stark white flooring, formed of reconstituted glass and seen as floating independent of its setting. Furniture is kept to a bare minimum: the cash desk is formed within one of the steel rail structures. At one time, high fashion courted architectural minimalism, seeing it as a good background for displaying the goods. Future Systems' work demands attention and is anything but minimal. Architecture and fashion merge to form a magic world – alas, one that may prove all too ephemeral.

Right and opposite
Future Systems' Marni store is extraordinary for its use of vivid colour and unusual materials (the floor is of reconstituted glass) and for its rejection of the customary shop fittings in favour of a system of steel rails and trees

PETER JONES, SLOANE SQUARE, SW3
JOHN McASLAN & PARTNERS, 1997–2004

The Peter Jones store is one of the few modern buildings in London that has been almost universally popular since the first phase of William Crabtree's scheme, with its great curving curtain wall on to Sloane Square, was constructed in 1935–37. Crabtree was rebuilding an existing department store. The Second World War brought work to a standstill, and elements of the Victorian building were retained when the project was eventually completed in the 1960s to a compromised version of the original scheme. Inside, some awkward spaces were created, with poor connections between departments, though the progressive outlook of the John Lewis Partnership ensured that staff facilities, which included a theatre and squash courts, were a priority.

John McAslan's phased £100,000,000 reconstruction aims to address the failings of the existing building and finally to realize the promise of Crabtree's extraordinary vision. Floor levels are to be rationalized, the disjunctions within the building addressed, and new servicing and storage areas created. At the heart of the store, a spectacular new central light well will rise seven storeys to the roof, with escalators serving all floors. Services will be entirely renewed, with a progressive energy strategy that makes use of chilled beams – for the first time in a British retail development – to cool the spaces. Existing façades will be seamlessly upgraded in line with modern environmental standards.

Externally Peter Jones will remain the modern landmark it has always been, but it will be re-equipped to retain its position as one of London's best-loved shops. This project sets a new benchmark for the sympathetic rehabilitation of classic Modern Movement buildings, all carried out with the store open to customers and within the context of a landlocked site surrounded by busy streets.

Right and opposite
The reconstruction of the Peter Jones store, a 1930s Modern Movement classic, provides a new full-height atrium with escalators serving all floors, and addresses the shortcomings of an awkwardly planned interior completed, to a compromised plan, in the 1960s

SAINSBURY'S, GREENWICH PENINSULA, SE10

CHETWOOD ASSOCIATES, 1996–2000

Back in the late 1980s, Sainsbury's surprised the world of food retailing by commissioning Nicholas Grimshaw to design its new branch in Camden Town. It was a bold move, though the interior of the store is a standard Sainsbury's fit-out of the period – as if the client's nerve had failed well into the project. Nonetheless, the development, including ten town houses and some workshops, provided a refreshing contrast to the sub-vernacular style favoured by other chains.

The store at the Greenwich Peninsula was bound to be seen as something of a demonstration project, given the high aspirations of the masterplan for the area. The aim was to produce a pioneering low-energy building. The store is rooted to the site by earth banks, piled against the thick concrete side walls, which have a structural function – supporting the dramatic arched roof beams – but equally act as insulation. The roof itself is heavily insulated, with double glazing applied to the north light that provides adequate illumination on all but the dullest days; artificial lighting is generally close to the shelving. Surplus heat and chill from the refrigerators is fed into 75-metre-deep boreholes for storage. Natural ventilation is supplied *via* an underfloor void, which carries all services. Vehicular servicing is from basement level, avoiding the untidy service areas that clutter most supermarkets.

The twin wind turbines that flank the entrances to the car park look like tokens, but the energy savings provided by the overall environmental package are significant: up to half on the typical demands of a conventional store of this size. It is easy to belittle the project as itself a token gesture, given the nature of the supermarket business, but it at least marks a step forward. Chetwood Associates' architecture is slick and of the moment, with none of the conviction of a Grimshaw but perhaps a closer understanding – from a firm with plenty of retail experience – of what shoppers like. The RIBA jury that gave it an award in 2000 considered it "an excellent building – full stop".

Above
Earth banks root the store to its exposed site and provide insulation to reinforce the progressive energy strategy of the scheme

Opposite
The shaded glass façade and roof lights provide plenty of natural light – artificial lighting is used far more sparingly than in a typical supermarket

FURTHER READING

Allinson, Ken, and Thornton, Victoria, *London's Contemporary Architecture: A Visitor's Guide*, 2nd edn,
London (Architectural Press) 2000

Anderson, Robert, *The Great Court and the British Museum*, London (British Museum Press) 2000

Casson, Hugh, *New Sights of London*, London (London Transport) 1938

Davies, Colin, *Hopkins 2*, London (Phaidon) 2001

Foster & Partners, *Foster Catalogue 2001*, Munich (Prestel) 2001

Future Systems, *Unique Building: Lord's Media Centre*, Chichester (Wiley-Academy) 2001

Hardingham, Samantha, *London: A Guide to Recent Architecture*, 5th edn, London (Ellipsis) 2001

Jackson, Alan A., *London's Termini*, Newton Abbot (David & Charles) 1969

Jencks, Charles, *Post Modern Triumphs in London*, Architectural Design Profile 91, London
(Architectural Design) 1991

Jones, Edward, and Woodward, Christopher, *A Guide to the Architecture of London*, 3rd edn, London
(Seven Dials) 2000

Lawrence, David, *Underground Architecture*, Harrow (Capital Transport) 1994

Lambot, Ian (ed.), *Reinventing the Wheel: The Construction of British Airways London Eye*, Haslemere
(Watermark Publications) 2000

McKean, John, *Royal Festival Hall*, Buildings in Detail, London (Phaidon) 1992

Moore, Rowan, *et al.*, Building Tate Modern, London (Tate Gallery Publishing) 2000

Nairn, Ian, *Nairn's London*, Harmondsworth (Penguin) 1966

Nairn, Ian, *Modern Buildings in London*, London (London Transport) 1964

Powell, Kenneth, *World Cities: London*, London (Academy Editions) 1992

Powell, Kenneth, *Richard Rogers: Complete Works, II*, London (Phaidon) 2001

Powell, Kenneth, *The Jubilee Line Extension*, London (Laurence King) 2000

Powell, Kenneth, *et al.*, *The National Portrait Gallery: An Architectural History*, London
(National Portrait Gallery) 2000

Power, Mark, *Superstructure* [a photographic study of the building of the Millennium Dome], London
(HarperCollins) 2000

Rogers, Richard (with Mark Fisher), *A New London*, London (Penguin) 1992

Rogers, Richard, *Cities for a Small Planet*, London (Faber & Faber) 1997

Sabbagh, Karl, *Power into Art: The Making of Tate Modern*, London (Penguin) 2001

Sudjic, Deyan, 'The Millennium Experience, London: A Dome, yet Different', in Rowan Moore (ed.),
Vertigo: The Strange New World of the Contemporary City, London (Laurence King) 1999

Summerson, John, *Georgian London*, London (Pleiades Books) 1945 (and many subsequent editions)

Towards an Urban Renaissance: Final Report of the Urban Task Force, London (E & F.N. Spon) 1999

Unbuilt London, special issue of *The Architectural Review*, January 1988

Wilhide, Elizabeth, *The Millennium Dome*, London (HarperCollins) 1999

Wilkinson, Chris, and Eyre, James, *Bridging Art and Science: Wilkinson Eyre Architecture*, London
(Booth-Clibborn Editions) 2001

PICTURE CREDITS

The illustrations in this book have been reproduced courtesy of the following copyright holders:

Adjaye & Associates.p. 157; Max Alexander pp. 196, 197; Allford Hall Monaghan Morris pp. 146, 147; Allies & Morrison p. 153; Alsop Architects pp. 56, 57, 103, 216, 217; Shigeru Ban Architects/Gumuchdjian Associates p. 24; Sue Barr p. 215; T.P. Bennett pp. 38, 39; Hélène Binet pp. 164, 165; Birds Portchmouth Russum p. 33; Sarah Blee pp. 162, 163; Hugh Broughton Architects p. 134 (top); Buschow Henley p. 220; Peter Campbell pp. 192, 193; Cartier pp. 228, 229; Cartwright Pickard Architects pp. 178, 179; Andy Chopping pp. 108 (right), 109 (bottom); Peter Cook/VIEW pp. 1 (half-title), 9, 11, 13, 16, 42 (top), 77 (top left), 111 (top); CZWG Architects p. 34; Kevin Dash Architects/Gumuchdjian Associates pp. 172, 173; Richard Davies pp. 97, 100, 101, 201, 213, 230, 231; Richard Davies/Hayes Davidson pp. 190 (bottom), 191; Jeremy Dixon: Edward Jones pp. 70 (top), 113 (top); Peter Durant/ arcblue.com pp. 82, 83; Courtesy English Partnerships/Henderson pp. 140, 141; Terry Farrell & Partners pp. 174, 175, 202, 203, 208, 209; Foster & Partners front jacket, pp. 30 (top), 60–61, 61, 73, 122, 123, 200, 218, 219; Fraser Brown MacKenna pp. 168, 169; Chris Gascoigne/VIEW pp. 6, 8, 17, 35, 95; Dennis Gilbert/VIEW pp. 10, 14, 21, 28, 29, 30, 31, 40, 41 (bottom), 44, 45, 46, 47, 51, 52 (middle and bottom), 53, 58, 59 (middle and bottom), 68, 69, 70 (bottom), 71, 76, 77 (top right), 89, 104, 105, 112, 113 (bottom), 128, 129, 130, 131, 138, 139, 154, 155, 234, 235 (bottom); Richard Glover/VIEW pp. 77 (bottom), 102, 235 (top); Nicholas Grimshaw & Partners Limited pp. 86 (top), 132, 133; Haworth Tompkins Architects pp. 108 (left), 166 (top), 167 (top); Hayes Davidson p. 96; Hayes Davidson/Nick Wood pp. 36–37 (bottom); Hodder Associates back jacket, pp. 90–91; Andrew Holt pp. 142, 143; Michael Hopkins & Partners pp. 59 (top), 212; Trevor Hornes/Inigo Bujedo Aguirre p. 23; Nick Hufton/ VIEW pp. 64, 65; Stephen M. Johns pp. 74, 75; Nicholas Kane pp. 126, 127, 180, 181, 182, 183, 221; Katsuhisa Kida pp. 204, 205, 224, 225 (bottom); Kohn Pedersen Fox p. 190 (top); Lifschutz Davidson p. 37 (top and middle); Benedict Luxmore pp. 66, 67; MacCormac Jamieson Prichard p. 50; Peter Mackinven pp. 48, 49 (top); Peter MacKinven/ VIEW pp. 80, 81, 98, 99, 148, 149, 212 (bottom); The Manser Practice p. 94; Nick Meers/VIEW p. 18; Marks Barfield Architects pp. 184, 185; Rick Mather Architects/ BDP p. 49 (bottom); John McAslan & Partners pp. 106, 107, 120, 121, 144, 145, 232, 233;

Miller Hare pp. 152, 210, 211; James Morris, Photographer pp. 134 (bottom), 135; Munkenbeck & Marshall pp. 158, 159, 170, 171; Andrew Putler p. 176 (top); Putler/3 DD p. 36 (top); Richard Rogers Partnership p. 225 (top); Sellar Property Group/Broadway Malyan pp. 206, 207; Grant Smith pp. 42 (bottom), 43, 160, 161; Grant Smith/VIEW pp. 194, 195; www.smoothe.co.uk pp. 86–87; Paul Smoothy pp. 186, 187; Snell Associates pp. 92, 93; Timothy Soar p. 52 (top); Morley von Sternberg p. 116; Swanke Hayden Connell pp. 222, 223; Paul Tyagi/VIEW pp. 2 (frontispiece), 138, 139; Victoria and Albert Museum, London pp. 78, 79; Philip Vile Photography pp. 109 (top left, middle and right), 118, 119, 166 (bottom), 167 (bottom); John Walsom pp. 114, 115; Alan Williams/ Wordsearch p. 214; James Winspear/VIEW pp. 54, 55; Charlotte Wood pp. 111 (bottom), 176 (bottom), 177; Nick Wood p. 88; Ken Yeang/HTA p. 156; Nigel Young p. 72; Nigel Young/Foster & Partners pp. 20, 30, 32 (middle), 198, 199

The publisher has made every effort to trace and contact copyright holders of the illustrations reproduced in this book; they will be happy to correct in subsequent editions any errors or omissions that are brought to their attention.